"A deep and ⟨...⟩ ɔm of
non-duality tɔ ⟨...⟩ aking
us through thɛ ⟨...⟩

—Tim F⟨...⟩ ⟨...⟩p Awake

"I've worked closely with Nic Higham for several years and have read his website posts about awakening with great interest and resonance. Working with Nic so closely over the years, I can assure you that his experience is direct. You can feel it for yourself as you read this book. It is my honor to introduce you to Nic if you aren't aware of his writings yet."

—**Scott Kiloby**, CEO of The Kiloby Center for Recovery

"Nic Higham's book is not only wise, but also deeply human, honest, and compassionate. Nic's own existential struggles with loneliness, isolation, forlornness, and angst were the portals to a more authentic Self that he has discovered and now shares in this book with great humility. Drawing on a wide range of wisdom teachings, including Nisargadatta's 'natural yoga' and what Nic calls 'radical mindfulness,' Nic examines separateness in a way that is spiritually, psychologically, and philosophically astute. Throughout this process of Self-remembrance, Nic skillfully reveals the essential Aliveness that is always at the heart of experience, and that is the source of greater harmony, wholeness, and connection."

—**Michael A. Rodriguez**, author of *Boundless Awareness*

"When we dive into the ocean of our aloneness, our loneliness can come to an end. What a beautiful paradox to meditate upon. In *Living the Life That You Are*, Nic Higham challenges us to stop running away from our present experience—however uncomfortable or intense it is—and plunge into the ocean of present-moment awareness. This is not about 'letting go of' or 'releasing' our anxiety, fears, and sorrows. This is not about destroying the ego or becoming a spiritually enlightened, super-human being, immune to the pains of being human. This is about being exactly as we are, human vulnerabilities and all. This is about letting go of our assumptions about reality and becoming deeply curious about ourselves, allowing our feelings instead of resisting them, watching our thoughts instead of trying to control them, questioning our beliefs instead of holding to them. This is about discovering the beauty in our ordinariness, the divine essence in our flaws, and coming to see that loneliness is not an enemy, or a mistake, or a sign of our failure, but a great signpost to non-dual awareness, a call to remember this constant, brilliant light that illuminates our lives from deep within. *Living the Life That You Are* weaves together psychology, ancient wisdom, and honest personal reflections into a coherent and inspiring whole. If loneliness is the great disease of the modern age, then Nic's heartfelt plea for self-love is much-needed medicine. Even if your mind cannot comprehend all the ideas contained within this book, your heart will know the truth of them."

—**Jeff Foster**, author of *The Wonder of Being* and
Falling in Love with Where You Are

"I've known Nic since 2011, when he first started working for the UK-based social justice charity of which I am a trustee. I have been deeply and consistently struck by his commitment, compassion, and creativity since day one. Nic's day job involves working to improve the lives and autonomy of the most marginalized social groups, with a specialist focus on mental health inpatient care. Having worked for many years in acute psychiatric wards and therapeutic groups, he is very mindful of the needs of those people who are particularly lacking in power, validation, and/or culturally reflective experiences. In the innovative projects he leads and contributes to, his approach is always to be palpably appreciative of professionals and their clients, and to write service development publications which are appealing, validating, practical, and easy to use. Although it is a different format and is intended for a different audience, *Living the Life That You Are* is informed by Nic's egalitarianism and his unique experience. The book has a simple but profound message: live meditatively and inquiringly through cultivating the bespoke selection of mindfulness principles offered. Start your inner revolution with radical mindfulness: when you feel separate from life, become your own best friend by shifting your focus of attention to your sense of being, a most loyal quality we all share. Nic shows readers how to locate and tap into this place to help them feel more connected with themselves and others. I cannot recommend enough the opportunity to bring his passion and experience to a wider audience."

—**Jonathan Jenkins**, chief executive of
London Air Ambulance

"At the heart of Nic Higham's meditative reflections on non-duality lies an invitation to deep self-inquiry. As any earnest seeker eventually realizes, life's deepest truths cannot be known or attained by the mind; rather, the truth gradually reveals itself to those willing to look behind the veil. Higham shows us that loneliness and anxiety—rather than being states we should attempt to overcome—can be portals into profound Self-intimacy. With kindness and clarity, he elucidates the qualities necessary for us to experience for ourselves what the phrase *non-dual* really means. As an experienced mental health professional, he has combined a deep understanding of both psychology and non-duality to create a work—both words and music—by which to guide us into the knowing we are all ultimately seeking."

> —**Fiona Robertson**, senior facilitator and trainer of Scott Kiloby's Living Inquiries, and author of *The Art of Finding Yourself*

"Nic writes well and has understood the teachings of Advaita. The book should work well as a guide and self-help (as opposed to Self, which needs no help!)."

> —**Maria Jory**, editor of *Beyond Freedom*

LIVING THE LIFE THAT YOU ARE

FINDING WHOLENESS WHEN YOU FEEL LOST, ISOLATED & AFRAID

NIC HIGHAM

New Harbinger Publication, Inc.

Publisher's Note

This publication is designed to provide accurate and authoritative information in regard to the subject matter covered. It is sold with the understanding that the publisher is not engaged in rendering psychological, financial, legal, or other professional services. If expert assistance or counseling is needed, the services of a competent professional should be sought.

Distributed in Canada by Raincoast Books

Copyright © 2018 by Nic Higham
                    Non-Duality Press
                    An imprint of New Harbinger Publications, Inc.
                    5674 Shattuck Avenue
                    Oakland, CA 94609
                    www.newharbinger.com

Cover design by Amy Shoup; Acquired by Jess O'Brien;
Edited by Melanie Bell

Library of Congress Cataloging-in-Publication Data on file

20   19   18

10   9   8   7   6   5   4   3   2   1

First Printing

Contents

PART 3: Alone with All: Natural Unity

Foreword

You've been conditioned to suffer. In other words, from the time you were a young child to the present moment, you were taught to think a lot and avoid or seek certain experiences. Even more detrimental to our well-being is the mind's tendency to evade presence and so obscure Awareness, which is always present and ultimately what we are. Thought has become our main way of experiencing the world, thereby giving us a false sense of identity and security. When loneliness, fear or anxiety, or any form of suffering comes up, our tendency is to go into our minds and disconnect from our direct experience. More than anything, we've disconnected from ourselves through trying to search beyond ourselves because we think that what we are is not enough. We look for the future to fulfill us, for relationships to make us whole, and for addictive substances and activities to medicate unwanted feelings. The mind doesn't realize that true freedom arises from mindfully observing and inquiring into what is present—both the pleasure and the pain—by questioning our assumptions and sense of deficiency. In this book, author Nic Higham skillfully shows us that the key to our freedom is actually found in and through the suffering we experience. For thousands of years, those who have gone deep into these realizations have been telling us that desire, fear, and illusion are the three pillars of suffering. As we dissolve these three pillars, we begin living exclusively in the present moment rather than in our heads and in the past and future.

Self-intimacy is what we are all looking for, even if we don't yet realize it. We've been looking in the wrong places for our joy and peace. It is already within us, waiting to be accessed. Everything is included in the life that we are—the entire world of phenomena—but nothing sticks to us, as Nic says. When we learn to live our lives within the flow of everything that is happening, without avoiding or escaping anymore, our suffering finds relief. Nic invites us not to attempt to relinquish anything but to make peace with what is, without trying to reach a final conclusion or ideal. I can't tell you how often I have seen suffering continue in people because of their desire to relinquish the suffering rather than to be with it and allow it.

Working with Nic so closely over the years and having read his blogs with great interest, I can assure you that his experience is direct. You can feel it for yourself as you read this book. He points again and again at how the mind cannot grasp this realization. We want so much to be able to understand or grasp presence. But, as Nic points out, presence (or what Nic refers to as Aliveness or Beingness) is merely the context in which everything—every thought, emotion, sensation, state, and experience—comes and goes temporarily. There is literally no concept to hold onto. And Nic doesn't give you any concept to sink your teeth into. Instead, his spacious and well-chosen use of words is here to point you to this direct seeing, which can reveal a great peace and well-being—far beyond anything the conceptual mind can grasp. The invitation to deeply investigate every assumption and idea about ourselves, others, and life is what makes Nic's approach so radical in my view. The reader is given very precise context for using the mindfulness tools presented in this book (the SEER CRAFTS), rather than being addressed directly from the realization itself, which often feels too advanced for people beginning this kind of exploration.

When you're reading any book about non-duality, the key is not to read in order to gain mental understanding, but rather to notice the tone, feel, and spaciousness of the presentation of the words. Anyone can write a book about being present. But it takes the direct experience of presence to actually express words that convey, instruct, and point to presence in a clear and helpful way. Nic repeatedly helps the reader rest and stabilize as that which is aware. This is the greatest gift, and really the only gift, a book on non-duality can provide. Nic uses a masterful choice of words to break open your heart and pull the rug out from under you at every level of your thinking. This is the sign of an author who is speaking from his heart and from his direct experience, rather than regurgitating concepts or trying to present himself as a teacher.

It is my honor to introduce you to Nic if you aren't aware of his writings yet. *Living the Life That You Are* is about unlearning all the suffering you've accumulated throughout your lifetime. And the great thing about this book is that it simply points to the Awareness that is reading these words right now. Nic points to it so directly, over and over, that you may just see for yourself that there is nothing to get. This can reveal that you are what is looking, and that this is what you've been looking for all your life.

—Scott Kiloby, author of *The Unfindable Inquiry: One Simple Tool to Overcome Feelings of Unworthiness and Find Inner Peace*

Introduction

To learn to see, to learn to hear, you must do this—go into the wilderness alone.

—Don José, cited by Joan Halifax in
The Fruitful Darkness

Alone, I looked around at the strangers sitting nearby: independent people walking and talking, going about their individual lives. And, to my amazement, I became everyone I saw. The man in the suit in a frenzy, bellowing commands at the phone pressed to his ear, his ruthlessness further widening the divide between him and his coworkers. The young couple coming to terms with the death of their time together, joined now only as they attend the postmortem and dissection of the corpse over a final coffee. The new mother besotted by birth, helplessly absorbed in tiny fingers, toes, and nursery rhymes. Her world, her universe, all that mattered, all that was, gazing right back at her. It all felt so familiar, so beautifully, painfully intimate. The ancient couple to my right holding hands across the table with mouthfuls of caramel shortbread, ridiculously rich in chocolate and undying romance, reminiscing with tears and smiles, reliving the good times of days gone by. All life was in that coffee shop, and I was in love with it. I was living it and it was living me. I was alone and at one. Yet just a few moments before, I was sitting by myself with a soy cappuccino in one hand and my self-consciousness in the other. Now, I saw myself in everyone and everyone in myself.

Have you ever wondered why you sometimes feel lonely or isolated, even in a group of familiar people? And then, paradoxically, why is time alone sometimes fulfilling and nurturing?

Like many people, you might think of loneliness as a negative experience, brought on by a lack of connection with others. You may also have a sense that loneliness mostly has to do with how we perceive and deal with the level of social isolation we face. Sometimes solitude is necessary and salutary, a respite from a world that's gotten too busy. More often, though, being alone feels peculiar and daunting and many of us do our best to avoid it if we can.

These feelings are all too familiar to me. Maybe they originate from being pushed out of a cozy womb way too early, for example: that stark shock of clinical exposure, gasping for air in alien arms, separated from my mother, attached to a machine in an incubator. I could list a million other possible causes—being a timid, irrelevant outcast at school, for example. But whatever the reason, isolation and loneliness have always been my worst best friends and their awkward loyalty has never waned.

I've realized that loneliness, isolation, and anxiety are not as clear-cut as they first seem. Their roots go far deeper than merely having too much stress or not enough social contact. Alternatively, realizing our *aloneness* can be a catalyst to reflect, to meet and understand ourselves, not just as people, but as a seamless part of life itself. To be clear, I'm not describing *solitude*—the state of being away from society by oneself as a *separate individual.* I'm pointing to the reality that we're ultimately not individuals but expressions of the One Life, and as such, unified with wholeness. Aloneness is synonymous with oneness. Such a radical realization can be both anxiety-provoking and awe-inspiring, and can unfold anywhere with or without others, just as I experienced in that coffee shop.

Fundamentally, the root of suffering is our perceived separateness from life, which means that we experience life through the eyes of duality. We're pressured from inside and outside ourselves to stand out from the crowd; "Be unique, do well, have more." In particular, we seek communion with others and we look for a sense of completion. Paradoxically, we also seek contentment in ourselves, to be at peace with a world that seems to be "out there." We try to achieve these aims while at the same time trying to heal the very separateness we're striving to establish. Therefore, this underlying bewilderment and isolation fuel our society's every pursuit: material, psychological, professional, social, and spiritual. Innocently, we're looking in the wrong places; assuming love, peace, acceptance—or whatever we're seeking to be complete—is out there; seeking somewhere, something, or someone else. It's our sense of disconnection that triggers this outward seeking. This agitated neediness only creates more division and suffering, bearing little fruit.

If this resonates with you, you're most likely ready to look deeper into your perception of these experiences of loneliness and isolation, and consider their root cause. Maybe you've tasted both the nectar of solitude and the ache of loneliness and you want to gain more understanding. These feelings are birthing pains for something greater. You're not alone. Or rather, you don't have to feel isolated in your quest.

Reexamining Separateness

Reexamining separateness is the heart of this book—it is a journey of discovery that I am sharing here, in these pages. We won't just focus on loneliness and isolation, but they are relevant experiences to explore because our encompassing sense of separateness has a powerful influence on our daily lives. For that reason, this book isn't for your self-improvement; it's a catalyst for your Self-discovery, or to put it even better, Self-remembrance (Self with a big "S" as distinct from the small egoic self). This book invites you to come to know yourself as inherently complete and flawlessly connected with your Source. Through radical mindfulness, you'll embrace a wider perspective by shifting and broadening your focus.

Thankfully, this is simpler than it sounds. This book will help guide you home, back to Self. In this way, spirituality doesn't redefine or improve a solitary person; spirituality wakes us up to the truth about ourselves.

The pages that follow use an informal and playful Self-remembrance approach, an approach which gradually presented itself to me on my bittersweet journey. Additionally, I'll give you practical, simple meditative inquiries designed to bring greater clarity. I call this approach "radical mindfulness," which is nothing other than the readiness to observe, acknowledge, and question our experience without censorship. Living this way, we refuse to be led by duality and deficiency. Instead, we find the courage to see, welcome, and work with all that comes our way, returning to the immediacy of what we inherently are even in our dualistic expressions.

Radical mindfulness will help bring you back to your essential Aliveness, to true connection, a Deeper Knowing. This isn't an intellectual exercise (although we'll use and acknowledge our minds for the remarkable tools they are) and it certainly isn't meant to be prescriptive. It's direct engagement with life, not analysis of it. It's an explorative meeting of your foundational Self, the same non-dual Source all the great spiritual teachers and texts have been pointing us to for thousands of years.

Parts of the Book

PART 1: Restless Inadvertence and the Perception of Separateness

In part 1 of the book, we'll investigate loneliness with fresh eyes and consider a new, radical perspective on aloneness. We look more at our apparent separateness, and I introduce the various "modes of life" I'll be referring to. We see how through "restless inadvertence"—the state of being switched on mentally but switched off spiritually—we've become seemingly cut off from life. Finally, we inquire into key aspects of our suffering: desire and fear, and we explore how imagination shapes our perspective on life.

PART 2: Shifting to a Discerning Focus with Radical Mindfulness

In part 2 we take a deeper look at anxiety and loneliness, and begin to encounter our essential Aliveness or Beingness. Finally, we explore the various aspects of radical mindfulness— the art of seeing ourselves with eyes of clarity and compassion as the One Life. I offer a set of mindfulness and inquiry qualities and skills for a more discerning focus, which I've arranged by the mnemonic acronym SEER CRAFTS: *Sincere curiosity, Embracing and releasing experience, Earnest questioning, Receptiveness to truth, Courage, Remembrance of Self, Attention, Fullness and emptiness, Tranquility,* and *Surrender.*

Each of the SEER CRAFTS have a musical depiction in the form of ten audio tracks. You can listen to these while reading, reflecting, inquiring, relaxing, meditating, or just anytime you need a radically mindful "soundtrack" to living the life that you are. Go to http://www.newharbinger.com/40859 to access these tracks.

PART 3: Alone With All: Natural Unity

In the final part of the book, we explore our natural unity with life in which we are deeply connected and harmonized with everything. Why is clarity so important and how can the SEER CRAFTS help us see clearly? We find out. We then get more of a handle on what it means to be radically alone and how this kind of aloneness is synonymous, not with isolation, but with oneness. Lastly, we discover that the final step beyond oneness is "Deep Knowing"—a profound, yet ordinary meeting with our indescribable, unlimited, eternal Self.

My hope is that you'll resonate with these words and tenderly listen to your own experience; this, after all, is the theme of our time together. If you take away just one insight, remember that your own Beingness (or Aliveness) is your most loyal companion. Beingness will walk with you on the pathless path to Self—the eternal Source of life. And so there is no reaching it, only realizing it. You are the way and you are the destination; there is nothing else to find except your Self. You are radically alone, at one with the fullness of life.

PART 1

Restless Inadvertence and the Perception of Separateness

CHAPTER 1

Seasoned by Loneliness, Awake to Aloneness

Our longing to live fully—from our beingness—calls us home to this natural presence. Our realization of truth arises from the lucidity of presence. Love flows from the receptivity of presence… All that we cherish is already here, sourced in presence. Each time we cry out for help, our longing can remind us to turn toward our true refuge, toward the healing and freedom of natural presence.

—Tara Brach, *True Refuge: Finding Peace and Freedom in Your Own Awakened Heart*

A patient I once cared for in hospital, a dying elderly man, lucidly shared with me his experiences of isolation, loneliness, and aloneness. "I've never felt so lonely," he began as he stared at the hospital room ceiling, motionless yet apparently moved by a sudden rush of intense emotion, "as when I've lost my own center of gravity and my life has been outward-looking toward other people, things, and events." He continued:

"Because of this I've lived with the emptiness of loneliness for many years, even when, especially when, my social and work diaries were full; while on my own and with others. But when I've found the right balance between my inner and outer life, when my eyes have been open to our vital bond, I've known real intimacy and unconditional love." He stopped for a few seconds and looked me in the eye pityingly before concluding, "So, loneliness will rob you, trick you, and teach you; solitary freedom is your only loyal companion, and lucky for you, he has bottomless pockets." What I believed this dear man was saying was that loneliness and isolation can reveal fruitful understanding when we stop trying to escape the discomfort they bring. Therefore, if we look under the surface, we might find that we're not separate from each other because we share the same expansive aloneness and profound connectedness.

Through the Eyes of Separateness

There are many ways to think about our human existence and to interpret our loneliness and aloneness. One study's findings on loneliness in later life suggest that loneliness is the subjective counterpart to objective isolation and the flipside of social support (Victor et al. 2000). This is the common perspective that loneliness occurs without a significant relationship, or is a response to a lost connection with a loved one.

Highly influential in our lives is a narrative of scarcity or the fear that we are lacking something both inwardly and externally. We have an intense (and at times very subtle) desire for a dependable bridge to unite our divided existence. Does this mean we're doomed to be forever hungry for more, and that we'll stay inside a defensive shell, removed from ourselves and others in solitary confinement? Desire and fear flavor our entertainment, politics, and culture and the messages they broadcast. Just turn on the news at any time or choose a random movie. Paradoxically, advances in technology have supposedly brought us closer together. Living in the "age of loneliness" was the subject of a 2008 study in which researchers found that up to one in five Americans suffers from chronic loneliness (Cacioppo and Patrick 2009). So, where *can* we find authentic connection?

Five million people regard television as their main form of company in the United Kingdom (The Campaign to End Loneliness 2014). What feelings do these findings evoke in you? Is connection the same as company? Have you ever had the television or radio playing in the background for company? I certainly have. It's so easy to fall into the well-trodden groove of avoiding our aloneness, loneliness, and anxiety, remaining asleep to a bigger perspective. But we can begin to rouse ourselves from our uneasy inattention by first turning away from distractions. Embracing our loneliness, we can use it as fruitful ground for greater insight and Self-remembrance—for Self-intimacy or Self-realization.

"The emphasis on conformity, following directions, imitation, being like others, striving for power and status, increasingly alienates man from himself," says Clark E. Moustakas in his delightful and seminal book *Loneliness* (1961), which explores existential loneliness. Because we're unable to experience life genuinely, or relate authentically to our own nature and to others, we often suffer from a "dread of nothingness." Loneliness, Moustakas says, is part and parcel of being, of existing, which, if embraced, can lead us to "deeper perception, greater Awareness and sensitivity, and insights into one's own being" (Moustakas 1961, 49).

While we fear specific things and experiences in the world (such as a fear of heights or public speaking), our anxiety is bewilderingly unspecific. Instead, anxiety, or more specifically, existential angst or dread, is the primary mood that shapes our relationship with existence (Panza and Gale 2009). In terms of existential angst, generalized anxiety is a reaction to freedom and an inescapable recognition of not-knowing. It becomes apparent when we reject convention and question the beliefs and ideas we've previously taken for granted.

When we assume that what we know is fixed and representative of truth, why investigate, especially if our fixed knowledge seems to serve us well? If it isn't, we feel unsettled, which means it's time to look beneath the surface of our conclusions. Existential anxiety forces us to inquire; it sets in motion purifying shifts of awareness, which unveil a new kind of freedom.

Shifting to a Discerning Focus

How did such a deep-seated sense of separateness occur? Because of our narrowed, distorted focus, we've become apparently disconnected from our essential Aliveness, which is universal. We are so accustomed to perceiving a dualistic paradigm; there's "me" and a world of "others" existing in an infinite and vastly unknown universe of disparate objects.

So I want to point you, firstly, toward your immediate and familiar sense of Aliveness or Beingness—that unmistakable resonance and knowledge of "I am" you know so intimately. Then I'll invite you to see that same, familiar Beingness/ Aliveness in all that is, including your body-mind. In this seeing, Aliveness becomes a kind of Deep Knowing or nondual Awareness, which is the end of separation.

The words isolation, loneliness, aloneness, and solitude are often considered to be synonymous. It's also true that these words carry a stigma. They send us the message that it's not okay to be alone, and that we must fill our lives with other people if we are to be happy, whole, and loved. Paradoxically, many of us have experienced loneliness even when with others, or have found comfort in aloneness. One thing is for sure, we want connection—real connection—and there are countless shades and nuances in the connection-isolation continuum. So what do we mean when we talk about being connected?

In her book *The Gifts of Imperfection*, Brené Brown defines connection as "The energy that exists between people when they feel seen, heard and valued; when they can give and receive without judgment; and when they derive sustenance and strength from the relationship" (Brown 2010, 19). This definition by itself, however, doesn't take into account another important form of connection: the connection we have with ourselves, and with the natural and manufactured world. But Brown offers a valuable clue which speaks to this: "How much we know and understand ourselves is critically important, but there is something that is even more essential to living a wholehearted life: loving ourselves" (Brown 2010, xi). Brown describes what she calls "Wholehearted Living" as an ongoing journey of cultivating courage, compassion, and connection, in which we learn to see ourselves as enough.

The Indian spiritual teacher Sri Nisargadatta Maharaj describes shifting the focus of attention and becoming the very thing one looks at, experiencing the kind of consciousness it has—oneness—and becoming the inner witness of the thing. He calls this capacity of entering other focal points of universal Consciousness "love" (Maharaj 1973, 269). As love, we are simultaneously everything and nothing; the seer and the seen are united. You may have moments when you've witnessed something striking—a piece of touching music, the tenderness or play of your children or pets, a beautiful landscape or object, the loving words of a stranger—whatever it is, it's your world for that instant. Giving your attention to it, you are absorbed in pure adoration and Awareness.

Maybe the relational energy that Brown describes and the all-embracing love Maharaj speaks of are the same. Perhaps the connection-isolation continuum depends on perspective—different ways of looking at the same life. And if so, can we learn to shift our attention to this energetic love?

Contemplate this: what you are (beyond the self-concepts) is boundless and all-inclusive. Marvel at the idea that you (beyond the confines of "me") are transcendent of time and space. Within that "you" that we call the Self, you arise as many focal points of universal Consciousness that project duality. Radical connection, then, can be revealed through putting things into perspective, through learning to "see" clearly and expansively. It is revealed by first connecting with our own Aliveness—localized consciousness, or Being; our basic sense of existing—and then coming to recognize that Aliveness is not divided into separate subjective egos. I call this kind of seeing "discerning focus." It's not possible to cultivate Aliveness because it already *is*. Having said that, we can develop a discerning focus and distinguish the universal Consciousness from the changeable activity of the mind and the world it imagines. Chapters 7 to 16 detail the ten skills and qualities of Self-inquiry and meditation that will allow you to do this.

Alone with All

You've inherited the belief that everything beyond your skin is not you or yours, that you're limited to, and by, your personal internal world and the body that imprisons it. You've claimed and lost certain objects and people as your own on your journey. Your "possessions" have become extensions of your sense of individuality, providing distraction from your deeper existential separateness but not curing it. Your belief in a boundaried identity grew stronger as you matured and individuated, while those around you reinforced your distinctiveness. You were given a name and your parents or primary caregivers co-designed your personality. From a young age, you've believed that you must strive to establish and uphold your unique place in the world. That's what you've been told. Our society considers these ideas to be the norm and stigmatizes any contrary notions, avoiding and rejecting them for fear of losing oneself.

When you mindfully consider it, do you find that everything beyond your skin is "other"? Are you limited to your private world and confined by your body? Is individuality a barrier? Can individuals really "touch" one another?

And yet, if we could genuinely touch another—if a profound, expansive intimacy could occur—wouldn't each person touching perish? Or better, merge and become one, like colliding and coalescing bubbles? Isn't that what love is? Isn't that the call of the lonely and the price they must pay to satisfy their cavernous hunger for unity and end the separateness they experience? Even while we long for this unity, we still stubbornly defend our individuality, our separate identity.

It's as if something in us knows we are not merely islands, but part of the universal mainland we struggle to find: a microcosm of a much greater macrocosm. Let's explore the potential of focus as a way to meet the dilemma of loneliness and aloneness. Specifically, we'll inquire how, as mortal islands floating in apparent isolation, we can shift our Awareness to the universal life. This is the heartbeat of authentic connection.

Aloneness is not merely a social predicament. It is our essential nature. What's more, it's a nature from which we are estranged. How? Because of lack of clarity, says Osho: "instead of seeing our aloneness as a tremendous beauty and bliss, silence and peace, at-easeness with existence, we misunderstand it as loneliness. Loneliness is a misunderstood aloneness" (Osho 2014, 74). Once we misunderstand our aloneness as loneliness, the entire context of our existence changes. Osho continues: "Aloneness has a beauty and grandeur, a positivity; loneliness is poor, negative, dark, dismal" (Osho 2014, 74). This means that in our unified aloneness, we lack nothing. It is ignorance of our foundational oneness that gives way to a sense of dualistic separateness. Our divided state is characterized by desire, which moves us to pursue something external continually, or to seek a peak experience. Fear, on the other hand, is another aspect of this divided state that causes us to avoid the experiences that might be challenging or unpleasant.

Because of desire and fear, which we'll explore in much more detail later, we misconstrue aloneness as loneliness. But if we're mindful and examine it in depth, aloneness can also be experienced as a capacity that's full of possibility, not a deficit in need of repair. Somewhat ironically, aloneness is something sacred that we share, whether in each other's company or physically by ourselves. This is an aloneness that, refreshingly and liberatingly, isn't characterized by the suffering we experience that comes with being identified as an individual body-mind.

With an open receptivity, you'll create space to summon an authentic existence. Discerning focus—which, remember, is a blend of skills and qualities of Self-inquiry and meditation—is not about gain, it's about truth, and sometimes truth can seem like loss. Discerning focus, radical mindfulness, is asking the question "What is true?" and being prepared for incomprehensible answers. Mindfulness means to focus Awareness onto what's taking place in the present moment. Yes, question everything, not necessarily to gain more answers but to release your assumptions. Question to make room for the light of truth to fill every part of your unlimited capacity.

CHAPTER 2

Through the Looking Glass of Separateness

If we understand that our sense of incompleteness is the result of having lost contact with our depths and that this contact is obscured by layers of psychological structure, it follows that all we have to do is to connect with our spiritual roots [and] thread our way back through these structures to what lies beyond them.

—Sandra Maitri, *The Spiritual Dimension of the Enneagram*

At 3:03 a.m. on August 8, 1983, I was born into isolation—I spent the first two weeks of my life in an incubator, creating a distance between me and those who loved me. As a child, I often felt lonely, because I saw myself as different from other kids. Feeling unsure of myself, I struggled throughout my childhood to find a place in the scary, big world. I was aware of a very subtle constant yearning to be embraced. I yearned not only to be lovingly held physically and emotionally but existentially, too—although I didn't have such words to express that deep desire. I wanted to find the comfort and nourishment of a womb-like space that would receive me, hold me, and tell me everything was okay without condition.

It was in my early twenties that my angst, and so my search, intensified and I discovered Buddhism and Hinduism, along with their extraordinarily enriching texts and practices. Was meditation what I was looking for? It certainly helped me to tune into something, some quality of equanimity, that was revealing itself in me and around me. But it soon became obvious that meditation was more of a signpost than a desti-nation. It was the words of the thirteenth century Japanese Zen Buddhist monk Dogen Zenji that sparked an energetic shift of focus. The words were, "Enlightenment is intimacy with all things." I was overlooking my essential nature.

By making friends with my yearning for wholeness and learning to inquire into the nature of myself and the world with greater focus and discernment, it became apparent that what I had been searching for was Self-intimacy. I now describe this profound intimacy as oneness or "radical aloneness"—which comes from reconnecting with our own Aliveness. Reconnecting in this way showed me that my true Self wasn't restricted to a body or personality, nor was it limited to the confines of time and space, and it couldn't be described or quantified. It was all things: the full breadth of life. I realized that I had always been alone, radically alone; not merely as an entity, but as life itself. The same applies to you. You too are the same life. I invite you to inquire with me into your present scope of self and to begin to gently push down the boundaries that contain and confine you.

Understanding Isolation and Loneliness

Before this shift (which wasn't as dramatic as it might sound), I had some very conventional ideas about isolation, loneliness, and aloneness. I believed they were nearly identical undesirable and unproductive states. On the contrary, each has its own unique character and resulting implications, and it turns out that sitting with and investigating each is both revealing and illuminating. The distinction among these experiences is not merely a matter of semantics, as you'll discover, and they certainly aren't synonymous. These experiences are linked because they describe how we relate to ourselves and others.

Most of us purposely reach out for companionship or relationship; it's what we do. We humans have always used social bonds and cooperation for survival through living and working together. This comes from our inborn tendency to seek out others to give us nourishment and love, to fulfill our needs, and for us to love, contribute to, and support. Social and health care professionals often see social integration and engagement as signs of a fruitful and healthy life. Indeed, it's widely believed that interpersonal support has a protective effect on our physical and mental well-being. This is most definitely true on one level.

In psychospiritual terms, our individual self is by definition deficient, because it has a life span and is dependent on other things that also have a limited life span. Identified this way, we use others as a means for self-enhancement; we try to find ourselves through our relationships. Similarly, we identify with our roles, status, and possessions, grasping for them and becoming preoccupied with scarcity, and a dread of losing our stockpile of ego embellishments. These embellishments, which are primarily adopted beliefs, are used to patch up a fragmented sense of individuality. We mold ourselves by inter-acting with the cultural framework in which we live and to which we contribute. Culture fashions the components of our sense of self and informs, to a large extent, our perception of reality. Right from our formative years, it gives us a way to communicate, to know what's acceptable, and to find meaning. Although it seems as if culture is "out there" somewhere, it exists in our minds as a bundle of recurring stories. These societal sound bites make up our collective character and codes of behavior. What this alludes to is a compelling experi-ence of individuality that is conceptually constructed, and seemingly alienated from the whole.

What are your cultural and societal beliefs? How are these linked with your various self-concepts? How might these play a part in your feelings of disconnection and inauthenticity? Maybe you feel you've been wronged by your culture or society, leading you to subscribe to stories such as "I'm a misfit," "I'm a wallflower," or "I don't have a place in the world." Perhaps you believe you'll never get the approval, love, acceptance, validation, and security you crave. However disconcerted your stories make you, bringing them to light means you've noticed your true nature has become distorted. Be honest with yourself. Own these stories, because their creation is an inside job and you're so much more than a story. Once this realization dawns on you, once you find your ever-present Beingness, your loneliness and isolation and the suffering they cause will lose their charge. When you inquire into your constructed world, not taking it as absolute truth, you'll see that it's an illusory sphere through which you filter your private and public experience.

Ego is preoccupied with desire and fear and fabricates a world of superior and inferior people; nothing frightens it more than emptiness and uncertainty. Ego's biggest fear is the realization of its illusory nature, a far worse death, it thinks, than the body dying. That is to say, believing in difference keeps it alive; its mission is to divide and conquer.

"There is no basic difference," was Sri Nisargadatta Maharaj's reply to a typical question asked by one of the many seekers who had traveled far and wide to Bombay to sit in the presence of this spiritual master: "Maharaj, you are sitting in front of me and I am here at your feet. What is the basic difference between us?" (Maharaj 1973, 3). Great though he was, Nisargadatta lived a modest and simple life up to his death in 1981, but his teaching, always delivered in a characteristically direct and uncompromising way, was extraordinarily profound. "I see what you too could see, here and now, but for the wrong focus of your attention. You give no attention to your self. Your mind is all with things, people and ideas, never with your self" (Maharaj 1973, 5). What Nisargadatta was pointing to (and what I echo in this book) is that our habit of inatten-tion and inadvertence causes us to lose sight of our underlying Beingness. Because of this distortion, we perceive a world divided into separate parts, making us view ourselves as fun-damentally isolated, incomplete, and insecure. Existence gets distorted by concepts and projections and from these springs the cycle of desire and fear: solitary confinement by way of an obscured lens.

Experientially, your body and individuality set you apart from other people and objects. This happens in a paradigm of relating and interacting as a human, which you might have experienced as interpersonal isolation and loneliness. On a deeper level, it's imagined duality which creates all manner of separateness—from the kind I call "dualistic isolation," the sense that you're identified with and alone in your body and your mind, to "existential loneliness," a persistent sense of incompleteness that no amount of social or material connec-tion can resolve. Bearing and inquiring into this alternative domain is a doorway to meeting our oneness. We'll explore this encounter and ways of shifting our attention to Beingness and oneness later. First, let's consider a typical understanding of the superficial form of isolation before we look at loneliness as a consequence.

Interpersonal Isolation

When I first left my family home, I shared a rented house with a close friend, who only lived with me for a short time. A few weeks after she moved out, my friend visited me to catch up and see to some financial loose ends. Glancing around the somewhat empty house, looking decidedly concerned, the first thing she asked me was if I was isolated. Her question took me aback somewhat because I hadn't ever stopped to reflect on how I felt. But she was right; I was isolated. My friend was able to quantify the level of interactions I was having and conclude it was likely that I was isolated. To come to this conclusion, perhaps she took into account the regularity, number, and quality of my relational connections, their robustness, and how I descriptively framed them, although I'm sure she didn't use such a checklist!

Interpersonal isolation, also called social isolation, is a state of total, or near total, lack of contact between a person and society. It's often a negative situation in which individuals, groups, or cultures experience a disconnect in communication or mutual support, often resulting in unease or even conflict. Because of these situations, the isolated face a loss of position within their networks and a yearning at some level for reintegration. An assortment of feelings arises. These include abandonment, rejection, loss, anger, marginalization, exclusion, frustration, sadness, meaninglessness, paranoia, apathy, loneliness, fear, and a desire for more contact with people who are valued.

Isolation can be both an unwanted consequence and a conscious action deliberately taken. Social isolation is a problem when it happens to us despite our wishes. And although we want to be alone sometimes, we also have a powerful impulse to be with others some of the time. We appreciate having provisional access to support, even if we choose not to tap into it. It's good to be part of something bigger than ourselves, to have a stronger voice and will, even to disappear in the crowd.

Interpersonal Loneliness

As isolation has two forms, so too does loneliness: interpersonal and existential. The former is the everyday kind, the experience of being isolated and the unpleasant psychological state it produces. We'll explore existential loneliness throughout this book.

Unlike social isolation, loneliness is a more subjective feeling of unhappiness we might have about the number (or quality) of our existing social connections. We can observe someone's isolation, but not their loneliness because it's an internal state. Conversely, we can only see the visible effects of loneliness, presented in another's words, behavior, and demeanor.

Many people experience an unbearable sense of emptiness when they're away from others for a while. In their secluded state, painful self-concepts emerge, and a dissonance arises between their inner and outer worlds as they resist the pain. Many people I work with who suffer from clinical depression tell me that boredom, silence, and aloneness are a toxic cocktail which dilutes vitality, energy, and optimism. One patient said her negative mental chatter, which told her she was inadequate and shameful, was loudest when not around others. As her experience illustrates, silence can be deafening. I've also heard loneliness described as murky, sticky, suffocating quicksand, which tries to pull one into itself, devouring hope. I wondered if this metaphor represents forlornness: the loneliness we experience when we realize that nobody can help us come to grips with comprehending our existence.

It can be terrifying to be cut off from human interaction. Being on the outside looking in undermines our self-esteem and self-confidence and erodes our sense of identity, therefore progressively breeding a fearful existence. Intense suffering arises from envisioning ourselves as unlovable and unacceptable. Fear, if left unresolved, reaps yet more isolation, and so more loneliness. In this way, loneliness repels opportunities for connection instead of attracting them, spawning a breakdown of interpersonal relationships.

Although it's true that isolation often leads to loneliness, loneliness is not, in itself, a prerequisite of interpersonal isolation. Both experiences can happen independently. This means it's possible to be lonely without necessarily being physically isolated. You'll know this to be true if you've ever been part of a group of family members, friends, or work colleagues and yet have felt confusingly cut off in their presence.

Being alone isn't always perceived as undesirable; we might voluntarily withdraw from others and spend short or extended periods on our own. When we consider alone time to be a positive decision, we usually think of it as privacy or solitude, the opportunity for personal or spiritual growth—or a much-needed rest. While writing this book, I went alone to see a show which was about a three-hour drive from my home. It so happened that my theater seat was next to someone else who was also traveling and attending by herself. As we both arrived early, we had some time to introduce ourselves before enjoying the show together as if we were old friends. After discovering we were both "loners," I listened with great fascination as Amy told me her story. "Being an only child, I've always been comfortable in my own company. Having a strong relationship with myself, I've never felt lonely, although I've been in some incredibly lonely situations—mostly when trying to fit in with peers. In my late twenties, I broke my femur in a serious accident and was admitted to a hospital far from home, away from my family, friends, and my boyfriend. Yet I still didn't feel lonely, not even in that clinical room without a TV, window, nor familiar faces. Fortunately, the extensive surgery, which at one point brought me very close to death, was a success. I felt lucky to be alive. Ironically, I only felt lonely when the man I loved came to visit me only to complain about the distance he'd had to travel. The kindest thing I could do for myself was to end that depressing relationship—it was a long time coming—and reconnect with myself more deeply. I've been happily single for two years, never once feeling lonely."

We can reconnect with and give attention to ourselves wherever we are and whoever we're with. We're not deficient in any way whatsoever, so there's no need to seek beyond ourselves—equality is the supreme order of things. This Self-intimacy can be transformative. It's this phenomenon which opened my eyes to there being another, more profound way of looking at loneliness, isolation, aloneness, and our deeper existence.

CHAPTER 3

Separateness Runs Deep, but Not That Deep

We are cut off from the great sources of our inward nourishment and renewal, sources which flow eternally in the universe.

—D. H. Lawrence, *A Propos of
"Lady Chatterley's Lover"*

Believing myself to be fundamentally separate has been a catalyst of great confusion and pain in my life. My loneliness, isolation, and forlornness have taught me a lot about myself and life when I've been willing to sit and listen to them. My own pain, that is, my humanness, coupled with my openness and curiosity, are my only real qualifications for writing this book. Though the road has not always been painless, my existential angst has served me well throughout my journey to return home. If you also find yourself lost, lonely, and afraid sometimes, know that these feelings are teaching you. Every insight is a gift of the unlikely marriage of pain and honesty, and you'll no doubt have many insights of your own.

A good place to begin is to recognize that loneliness and isolation aren't just brought on by the lack of a healthy social life, or anything we lack. If truth be told, we're under the spell of a much more fundamental and illusive sort of isolation. Such feelings are rooted in seeing life through the distorting filters of desire and fear—desire causing us to crave things we see ourselves as lacking, fear expressed as avoidance and defensiveness. Paradoxically, even our search for intimacy may be the reason for such feelings.

It might sound like a cliché, but we're always looking for ourselves, our truest selves. And while it may at first seem incongruous in our search for connection, what we're actually trying to find is our deeper Self—our infinite, non-conceptual Self, with a capital S. Looking more deeply beneath our identity, we find that it's the same Self that is everyone. This Self is the all-encompassing, undivided Self that is everyone and everything. In this exploration, we'll discover that it's Self-alienation and estrangement that compel us to avoid interpersonal separation and loneliness.

Our Underlying Sense of Disconnection

By the conventional definition, you're a separate and finite individual in a world of otherness, but all definitions are open to interpretation and scrutiny. It seems that your body and mind, thoughts, feelings, memories, and hopes are yours and unique to you. This is what I call "dualistic isolation," the product of our compelling belief in duality and separateness.

In short, a dualistic mind sees a world divided into subjects and objects, as that is how we've traditionally divided up life. In this state, our narrative is: "I want to be somebody or something. I want to be unique and stand out, but I want to blend in and be accepted, as well." Being an individual in a time-bound body means being different, so loneliness and isolation characterize the human condition, and it's as though real intimacy is out of reach.

In this sense, social estrangement and loneliness are just two symptoms of disconnection. In fact, I'd go as far as saying that dualistic isolation is the root cause of the world's suffering. It underpins our constant struggle to find some distant happiness, or to hang on to something that seems to give us fleeting moments of enjoyment, and our fight against what threatens that happiness or enjoyment. This seeking and resisting only serve to perpetuate our Self-alienation. Unknowingly, we get lost in this push-pull tug-of-war, or more precisely, we lose ourselves in it, and we can't find lasting peace and fulfillment. Even when we don't realize it, we're looking for a direct relationship with reality—the authentic Source of belonging and love. We suffer from misidentifying ourselves as separate beings and from seemingly having no roots in the ground of Aliveness. We rarely look into or question the validity of our underlying disconnection because we're asleep to it. Instead, our focus is usually on the surface of our everyday, habitual lives. We often take separateness for granted without questioning the validity of the appearance.

Our perspective is narrowed and distorted by desires and fears, most of which we've inadvertently absorbed from our culture. A significant story for me was that other people (especially strangers) could pose a physical or emotional threat. Wherever I was, I habitually anticipated this difficult experience by trying to make my body small, becoming contracted and recoiled. I was like a frantic armadillo that, failing being able to escape by burrowing into the ground, did the second-best thing and rolled up into a tight ball. Over time, holding my body in such a way took its toll, and my muscles became painful and tense. On top of this, I was overwhelmed with self-diminishing internal dialogue, and intense feelings of embarrassment became the norm for me. Ultimately, I wanted to shrink or conceal my existence before someone destroyed it. At the same time, I desired to be genuinely seen, heard, and known in my entirety, but, conflictingly, I feared the intimacy that such an encounter would demand. I desired survival over authenticity. When my suffering intensified, I became curious about it and started to question my assumptions. Through meditative inquiry, I came to understand that my fear of annihilation was totally unfounded and that limiting my sense of Aliveness was the exact opposite of what I needed to do to feel safe and connected. It's often only when we reach a crisis point that we start asking deep questions about our existence.

My seeking has taken all of the usual forms in more than three decades, and has led to various psychological and spiritual endeavors, which I once arrogantly considered to be the most sanctified means of seeking of them all. Subsequently, I was left with the same old questions and a lot more not-knowing, but something was comforting and familiar about my empty hands—and that presented a clue. With inquiry, I found that I was stuck and cut off by my own habitual inadvertence and narrow-sightedness because I was in the habit of taking so many things for granted. So I began to question attentively and honestly with an open mind, but to do so I had to be willing to encounter my existence in its overwhelming disconnectedness and expansiveness.

Breaking Free from the Cycle of Restless Inadvertence

I hope you're aware of your sense of existential separateness, even just a little bit, and that it suitably unsettles you. I hope you yearn for authenticity and connectedness. I trust you're open to inquiring into your dualistic isolation and that you're starting to find the willingness to let go of what you take to be true. Suffering calls for us investigate. And although perceived separateness is a fundamental part of human life, so too is your capacity for connection and tranquility. You don't deserve to suffer unnecessarily any longer. And as you become intimate with your Self, you'll be freed from the bondage of isolation and Self-alienation and begin to live with an outlook of loving, discerning focus. In radically mindful Self-intimacy, the misconceptions of separateness, scarcity, and vulnerability gradually dissipate.

What follows is a list of key words and concepts and their synonyms we'll be using to describe and understand our Self throughout our inquiry:

Modes of Life

1. **Self** (capital "S"): The Non-dual, Absolute, Deep Knowing, Awareness, Source, the Ultimate, truth, uncaused, infinite, indescribable, beyond time and space, supreme reality, all-exclusive and all-inclusive, the common ground of every experience, that which makes the following concepts possible and knowable

2. **Oneness**: Universal Being, universal Consciousness, universal witness, wholeness, all-inclusive love, impersonal existence, the sense of being deeply connected with all, the "**radical aloneness**" we all share

3. **Aliveness**: Beingness, Being, localized consciousness (immediate as opposed to universal), "I am," "I exist," sometimes experienced as "**existential loneliness**"

4. **Separate self** (small "s"): Person, individual, ego: "I am someone/something"; "I need other people and things to be whole." This self-image is based on an underlying belief in "**dualistic isolation**" which takes the superficial, experienced forms of "**interpersonal isolation**" and "**interpersonal loneliness**"

The "Separate self" mode of life is a product of:

◉ **Imagination**: The projected universe of time and space which projects Being through the following filters to give it form and meaning

◉ **Fear,** or "fear filter": Aversion, resistance, avoidance—suffering in the form of trying to push away a perceived threat

◉ **Desire**, or "desire filter": Scarcity, lack, grasping, deficiency—suffering in the form of trying to pull at something perceived to be an enhancement to the sense of self

Can you remember the last time you felt at one with life? What were you doing? What was your quality of Being? It's very likely that you were engrossed in something or someone you love or were curious about and you had some inner calm. You felt truly alive and free. The opposite state is "restless inadvertence." We get caught in perpetual cycles of restless inadvertence, as I illustrated above with my armadillo experience. When we lose sensitivity and attention, we get stuck and consequently overlook our expansiveness. This begins with imagining ourselves to be deficient ("I want," "I need," "I lack"), insecure ("I fear," "I can't bear," "I must resist"), and isolated from existence. We try to resolve this disconnect by seeking out people and possessions, but this results in more Self-alienation and suffering.

Radical mindfulness, instead, is the way to Self-intimacy—locating and continually returning to our Aliveness and our shared radical aloneness, the loving oneness of life, which unveils the indescribable non-dual Source that we are. Discerning focus embraces and releases our existential loneliness, expands our mindfulness, and reconnects us to our Self.

The "modes of life" model I present above might at first seem to reduce our rich human experience to a simplistic formula. This is just a way of attempting to describe our seemingly complex condition. I don't pretend that it's flawless, nor am I under the illusion that it perfectly summarizes our existence. No model could ever capture or begin to fathom the mystery that you are. But since books and minds rely on frameworks and ideas, I think this approach is as good as any, and, ultimately, it aims only to reconnect you with your Self, in which there is true peace and love. It's likewise worth pointing out here that the modes of life (as an interpersonal self, and as Aliveness, oneness, and Self) are meant to be descriptive rather than prescriptive; they aren't linear steps, stages, or levels toward reaching your Self, but merely an illustrative way of bringing clarity to our sense of isolation and showing the insight that's possible.

Facing our fundamental incompleteness or lack of wholeness—our existential loneliness—can offer an invitation for deep contemplation. Although it seems uncomfortably unresolvable, it offers the possibility of a transformative breakthrough. Existential loneliness is a symptom of imagined separateness, a very human story characterized by desire and fear. The yearning for wholeness provokes our loneliness.

Loneliness flavors existence, but if we embrace it mind-fully, it will reveal our connection to the infinite fullness of life. This kind of aloneness is not an experience of lack or deficiency; it offers a deep insight into our fullness. In radical aloneness, we directly face the crisis of separateness and question it. Through our willingness to hold and release whatever arises, including any sense of loneliness, we awaken to a transformative truth and love. Through awakening to this truth and love we learn that we are, and have always been, all-pervading, intimately one, radically alone. We awaken to an enriching and comforting communion with all.

Your Invitation to Self-Intimacy via Radical Mindfulness

Beneath the stories about who you are, where you've been, and where you're going is a deep receptivity which is both creative and accepting—it is the fundamental Source and also the unconditional embrace of your stories. It's what I call Deep Knowing: an all-encompassing Awareness that holds every experience including our Beingness. The primary quality of this Self-awareness is love. Not the desperate, lustful love, or the romantic ethereal love we read about in fiction, see on TV, or hear about in music, but love itself. Given earnest focus, pure Awareness, a nonintellectual knowing, comes to the surface naturally.

This is your invitation to turn within and find that what you thought belonged only to the outer world has its foundation inside your localized consciousness, the ground of Aliveness you already know so well. Then, in the space of mindfulness, non-dual Awareness will reveal itself to you as your all-pervading and ever-present companion. However, through mindful Self-remembrance you won't gain something new or realize a distant goal. You will, however, continue to be the incredible, unlimited life that you always were and always will be. That's more than enough, I promise you. This mindfulness will help you lucidly return to and connect with your Self repeatedly. Fortunately, Self is always present; only you habitually attach to things that distort your vision—body, mind, emotions, thoughts, beliefs, possessions, and the like, giving you the perception that you're a vulnerable, relatively small entity.

Loneliness runs deep—it's part and parcel of the human condition. Don't turn away from it, because it offers you the chance to blossom into what you are. A shift in attention to radical mindfulness is what's needed to see beyond your limited expressions to the whole. The lonely person is a phantom, a mere shadow of your entirety. This shift (which is more of an unraveling) may be instant, gradual, or intermittent. There are no right or wrong methods or outcomes of this unraveling, but we'll explore some key principles, qualities, and skills of radical mindfulness. Above all, everything you need is already within you, so your inquiry begins with meeting yourself exactly where you are with a heart of love and wonder.

CHAPTER 4

Imagination Constructs; Desire and Fear Shape

As human beings, we suffer from the problem of self—that is, of seeing ourselves cut off and isolated in a world of other things. This leaves us full of wanting and craving and fearing and loathing. Nevertheless, we all have the capacity to see with the eye of nonduality, with an eye that can penetrate thoroughly and completely the Totality of life. We can experience the world as a Whole.

—Steve Hagen, *Buddhism Is Not What You Think*

Everything begins with imagination. As we perceive life, we instantaneously intellectualize it and therefore distort it. The creative storytelling power of imagination projects color, shape, form, and meaning on the blank screen that is your primary nature. The moment you have a sense of Aliveness and you say "I exist," the entire universe is created, including your distinctive self-identity in contrast to other individuals.

This means that you don't exist because the world exists; the world exists because you do! Raw data get filtered through your conceptual model of the world, a world that's made of a bundle of ideas, desires, and fears. What you see around you reflects your self-conditioning, your repeated patterns of thoughts, feelings, memories, and habits. Out of restless inadvertence, the state of being switched on mentally but switched off spiritually, you've become split from the world you created and unfamiliar with your non-dual depths. Imagination is the catalyst of this dualistic isolation, and the resulting interpersonal isolation and loneliness are what cause you so much unhappiness.

Because you don't realize that you're viewing the world through imagination and that Aliveness is the animating light within your projection, you don't recognize that the world and your Aliveness are in fact one. Aliveness and the world are interrelated; there just seems to be a split between inner and outer experience, identifying with and fashioning your body-mind as the "inner" and believing that the world around you is the "outer."

Self-identification with your perceived body-mind has constructed division where there isn't any. Each conventional, yet fanciful, notion has an opposite—up and down, good and bad, night and day, past and present, cause and effect—but really, each opposite creates and cancels out its counterpart. The opposites are entirely malleable. If I were to sit opposite to you, for example, my left would be your right and your right my left. Perception is informed by perspective, which depends on the creative play of imagination. Giving this some contemplation, it becomes easy to see that the dualistic time-space world has a dreamlike quality, like that of a movie. There are subtle contradictions which can uncloak what's beyond the dream.

One thing you can be completely sure of, with a little introspection, is your vital Aliveness which underlies and illuminates the constructions of imagination. Aliveness precedes imagining. It's crucial to find and keep coming back to your Aliveness. Otherwise, you'll continue to experience isolation and alienation from life, from yourself. Make your Aliveness (Beingness, localized consciousness, I-am-ness, or whatever you wish to call it) your focus of meditation. With a commitment to remembering, this "coming back" surrenders the mind's storytelling, analyzing, and judging. The qualities and skills of radical mindfulness (explored in chapters 7 to 16) will give you the tools of discerning focus to do exactly this; imagination will become less dense and less compelling when you start to investigate. Your basic sense of Being is your gateway to unconditional reality, to true unity as pure Awareness.

When stepping into the threshold of this gateway, you may feel existentially lonely. Not only are you mindful of your presence, but you have a gnawing sense that your presence is a part of a much bigger whole. Existential loneliness is, therefore, a valuable and enriching state if embraced because it engenders contemplation and inquiry which moves us forward to find our fullness. On the other side of the gateway we may experience "radical aloneness," which is Awareness—the

Deep Knowing of and unity with that bigger whole, sometimes called "oneness." The absolute Self, which is beyond even oneness, is *one without an other*.

What you are in the truest sense is not a creation of imagination and therefore cannot be named or grasped. You can only be. You are Being it now. Even your sense of Aliveness, though a helpful provisional pointer, is but a reflection of your infinite Self. Let the emergence of your Self be your greatest desire, your deepest urge.

Because of its powerful effect on our narrative and outlook, it's worth spending some time exploring desire, along with its counterpart, fear. Desire is deeply rooted in us. It's what makes us curious about discovery and hungry for fresh understanding. It's what connects people and what helps us achieve the impossible. On the one hand, desire inspires in us our childlike wonder and our innocent playfulness, and on the other, it makes us childishly greedy and egotistical. Desire has a very close working relationship with fear, although they don't always get along. In a desiring state we yearn for experience, while in a fearful state, we resist experience. In this way, desire and fear are polar opposites of the same force: desire pulls, fear pushes. When you have a desire, you find a fear, and vice versa. Fear leads to desire and desire to fear.

Desire

Before even imagination, desire was the principal "Big Bang." It's a mystery why or how such a powerful explosion of passionate desire developed out of unspeakable completeness! One can only wonder: "Life desired, therefore I am." Thus, in partnership with imagination, it created your personal world along with your hopes and fears and everything in between. Desire taunts: "You must be something special and particular. Too much is never enough." In the face of sufficiency, desire laughs. In equanimity, it provokes imbalance.

I think of desire as a magnetic pull which makes the body and mind feel restless, penetrating much of our thoughts, feelings, and behavior. This infiltration fashions a profound sense of deficiency and expectancy in our identity as a separate self.

It was desire that gave birth to the body with which you identify. It was desire that gave you a name and a unique character. It was desire that led you to this book. It is desire that is calling you toward authenticity and Self-realization. Conversely, feasting on desire, the individual is nourished and ceaselessly left pining for more.

Desire is invariably both productive and destructive. Those of us whose lives have been touched and at times devastated by addiction—whether our own or someone else's—know all too well the creative thinking that gets what's needed to satisfy the craving, whether it's a substance or a process addiction. What psychologically motivates us in an addictive state are narratives of desire ("I need a fix to feel complete") and fear ("I can't face not having a fix"). Desire leads to fear and fear leads to desire. We could say that the primary compulsion is for self-concepts—to be someone or something distinct. Some people would rather die than lose all sense of who they are, or live with an unwanted self-concept, while for others, loneliness itself is like death.

Don't fight desire; just direct it mindfully toward your Aliveness, and let this focusing be a stopping place that leads to greater awareness and ultimately, to indescribable authenticity. Your greatest desire is to Be: every micro desire aims at the macro desire of authentic Aliveness. Try this short exercise to see this truth for yourself.

Focus your attention on one of your desires. You might visualize it as an object, person, or symbol. Ask that desire what its highest hope is. Keep repeating that question to whatever "answer" comes to you until you arrive at a quality such as love, peace, freedom, or joy. These are qualities of Aliveness which you already have. You can stop at this point or continue questioning until you reach a state of "no-mind" or "no-thought" where there's no longer an answer but a sense of Deep Knowing.

Here's an example:

I want people to like me. I see an image of others smiling and saying nice things about me. Upon asking what that desire's highest hope is, I get the words "to be accepted." Now, I'm focusing my attention on those words. What is the highest hope of "to be accepted"? The answer comes: safety; I want to be complete safe. What is the highest hope of this desire? Survival. What is the highest hope of this desire? To express myself. What is the highest hope of this desire? Love.

Fear

In overlooking our Self, we rely on things and people to make us happy and secure, and we go to war with, resist, and avoid the things and people that make us unhappy and insecure. As with desire, the target of fear is always in memory and anticipation, past and future.

In her book *Hidden Treasure: Uncovering the Truth in Your Life Story*, Gangaji offers this inquiry on fear. I've paraphrased her original words below:

> When in fear, see if you can stop depending on your conceptual knowledge of fear. Without knowledge, what is the experience? If you experience, for example, a body with sensations and you don't label or even know "body," what is experienced? (Gangaji 2013, 66)

When we ask these questions and follow our attention beneath our assuming and categorizing, says Gangaji, we're inquiring. Such direct experiencing bestows fresh, original insight. When we're willing to stop thinking about fear and directly experience it instead, we discover freedom. Without the label "fear," we discover an energetic force field which we've used to distance ourselves from life, made of the same benign essence as life.

Fear emerges because we're so powerfully led to believe we're self-contained and different from others. Fear is associated with a state of alertness, for "fight, freeze, or flight" and neurochemicals released in a potentially dangerous situation. Even babies, before they can talk or conceptualize, are fearful of loud noises and falling. Our psychosocial conditioning sometimes transfers this feeling of threat to other situations where we may not be physically endangered. However, our fears are often not in proportion to real danger, but a response to imagination gone wild, to ego insecurity. We pull people and possessions toward us to feel safe, but attachment and clinging only ever bring more instability.

When I talk about attachment, I don't mean the secure emotional bond between a child and a caregiver which is essential for healthy human development. By attachment I mean clinging, grasping, and neediness, which are far from conducive to a healthy state of mind. What we have, we'll lose, because everything is transitory. We live in denial of this universal fact. Such a disposition consequently drains much of our energy. We have fear that is not related to immediate or past threats of danger because we construct ourselves from impermanent sources and we imagine ourselves to be dualistically isolated. Fabrication and alienation breed trepidation. Our bodies are so fragile and susceptible to disease and damage, and even though we know that death is always around the corner, we still invest our ultimate identity in those bodies. Our very existence infers our extinction and our primal fear is of impending doom.

In loneliness, the immediacy of our essential Aliveness seems as though it isn't enough to put us at ease or to keep us grounded. Indeed, being in and bearing our own company can sometimes be intolerable or too close for comfort. We are closer to nothingness in solitude; we bring to light our otherwise shrouded mood of existential anxiety, which is related to fear but is not fear, per se. Whereas fear has a psychological or physical focus, existential anxiety has an existential focus (though existential anxiety may produce similar "stress" biochemicals as long-term exposure to physical or psychological danger). When we're no longer alone, the fear inherent in loneliness may subside, but anxiety follows us, which is why we may sit with isolation in the company of others.

Imagination is the apparatus by which we experience our I-Amness—"I exist." The light of Aliveness filters through desire and fear—figments of experience particular to the body-mind, which reinforces individuality. Aliveness is shaped by these filters into varying versions of the concept "I must exist as something or someone," and perpetuates the projecting. Seeing through a divided mind contracted by the pull of desire and the push of fear, we experience the world in the same dualistic way, which, if we're not mindful, leads to suffering. The energetic pushing and pulling of suffering is a *law of motion*, that for every action there is an equal and opposite reaction.

Desire and Fear Can't Yield Connection

We rarely see that the parts of life we favor wouldn't exist without their "complementary" aversions. This is the play of duality. It's what gives life color, texture, and meaning. Therefore, it's not diversity that causes our suffering but our attempts to pursue one oppositional extreme—either *yin* or *yang*, not both. Yin and yang, however, are seamless counterparts and perfectly embodied by their context. In fact, objects are inseparable from their context. Space is nothing—inconceivable—without an added object, however minute. Likewise, an object requires a background to exist.

With a radically mindful perspective, human experience no longer defines us. Instead, it celebrates our abundant potential. Being a person or a body is fine, but limiting ourselves this way is based on a deep-seated misunderstanding. In truth, the sum of existence, every expression, is ours, and arises within the fullness of the life that we are. We can recognize this with radical mindfulness.

PART 2

Shifting to a Discerning Focus with Radical Mindfulness

CHAPTER 5

Angst Is at the Threshold of Being

Life begins on the far side of despair.

—Jean-Paul Sartre, cited by Benedict
O'Donohoe in *Sartre's Theatre: Acts for Life*

As long as I can remember, I've had an underlying feeling of angst which has subtly pervaded every nuance of my life. If you've watched the movie *The Matrix*, you may understand how I related to the chilling wake-up call Morpheus offered to Neo as he was beginning to question reality: "What you know you can't explain but you feel it. You've felt it your whole life, felt that something is wrong with the world. You don't know what, but it's there like a splinter in your mind, driving you mad." This "splinter" finally leads Neo to the source of the Matrix program, the origin of his reality, where he subsequently initiates a master reset and brings about peace and harmony. The movie is a powerful yet disconcerting portrayal of our world. Many people agree that there's something bewilderingly incongruous about our existence; at times it's as if this not-okayness stems from the state of our politics, economics, or an environmental, social, or religious cause. Some people, like Neo, courageously follow their curiosity and try to get to the deeper root, seeking to unravel the raw fabric of reality beyond its visible forms.

For me, this existential malaise has shape-shifted into various elusive forms, all of which lacked a definable trigger or target. These forms could be called existential loneliness, existential depression, existential guilt, existential despair, existential insecurity, and predominantly, existential anxiety.

Existential Anxiety

As is the case for most of us, I've had an array of seemingly normal fears. But this other kind of anxiety was more like a quiet, unintelligible terror, a distant alarm bell, an uncaused danger. It seemed more real and fundamental than any passing concern. Apparently arising from my innermost core, existential anxiety was a lurking, menacing mythical figure. It hid in the shadows of my very Being, coming at me from everywhere and nowhere. It wasn't an entity but an inescapable mood that cunningly evaded reason and remedy. It was a constant undercurrent, an impending nothingness and hollowness, a strange intimacy with an enticing void, the cost of having a thumping heart and a free spirit. No, this universal anxiety (as opposed to generalized anxiety) didn't incarcerate me. Quite the opposite; it was a reminder of my choiceless freedom whispered incessantly, a peculiarly comforting promise.

Because existential anxiety was neither thing nor figure, I gradually learned that my instinctive fight-flight-freeze response to simple fears was useless when trying to confront or escape this deeper dread. Anticipating its elusive quality further intensified my anxiety. Helplessly, I couldn't ever evade this angst because it came from deep within me; it was a condition of my existing. I wasn't always conscious of it, at least not on a thinking level.

For years I thought I was alone in sensing this previously nameless dread. I was almost relieved to learn that it has been known to human beings since the emergence of self-consciousness: it has been explored and thought about throughout the ages. Although many have attempted to explain it, there's no genuine way to do so. Explanations rely on cause-effect formulations, and this existential malaise, along with its manifestations such as existential anxiety, has no intelligible cause. Unlike our fear-based problems, we cannot cure our illusive angst because it's not an emotional response to a measurable threat. Explaining a problem, searching for its cause, is a way to solve a psychological problem. Such methods do nothing for our underlying angst. This is our existential predicament.

Søren Kierkegaard, the nineteenth-century "father of Christian existentialism," sought to approach anxiety from the inside and described it as the "dizziness of freedom" (Thompson and Rodgers 2015). Existential anxiety, he suggested, occurs when we face the unknown coupled with the recognition of our own liberty, and so freedom tries to cling to finiteness to support itself (Kierkegaard and Hannay 2015). Kierkegaard saw anxiety not as a symptom of psychological ill health treatable with medication, but as a normal manifestation of human consciousness and freedom. We can think of existential anxiety as the non-psychological twin of fear. Whereas fear arises from *living as a human in the world*, anxiety stems from *living as a human*, which—let's face it—can be pretty perplexing at times. Learning to become acquainted with this anxiety is an adventure. Thomas Merton, the twentieth century Trappist monk, theologian, and mystic, wrote about the "dark night of the soul" in which we embark into darkness and meet inexorable forces (Merton 2005). In this "fire of purgation," we have to embrace fears and doubts. We are compelled to inquire deeply into the entire fabric of our spiritual life and must call forth the profound power in and as our very Being—our Aliveness. Albeit terrifying and beyond our comprehension, the dark night is a gift, said Merton, given to us moment by moment. If we reject this gift, the darkness grows ever blacker.

Existential Loneliness

As another manifestation of existential malaise, existential loneliness is an underlying condition of our existence. Just as psychological fear is usually temporary and existential anxiety is permanent, when our relationships improve interpersonal loneliness subsides, but existential loneliness lasts. When we're existentially anxious, we're alert to both the boundless nature of our essential Aliveness and the finitude of our present manifestation as a human being. Because we've mistakenly identified as an interpersonal self residing in a fragile body, we're dualistically isolated and therefore existentially incomplete and unfulfilled. In light of this realization, we yearn not for more friends nor the perfect romantic partner, but for the wholeness of our Being. Friends and partners bring only interpersonal relief, a relief which is characteristically inconsistent due to the variability of human relationships, but sooner or later existential loneliness emerges again.

Since it's a fragmented state of Being, our personhood and everything it implies make us existentially lonely. We feel divided from the whole of reality, as if we'll never be able to authentically participate with the universal. We experience the pain of living, of Being, and the prospect of dying as a singular entity. The existential psychiatrist, Irvin Yalom, says the loneliest event of life is death. Not only does death disconnect us from others but it also reveals another, even more horrifying kind of loneliness: the ultimate parting from the world itself (Yalom 2008).

Darkness Can Lead to Light

Being willing to no longer fight nor anesthetize ourselves, being brave enough to bring mindfulness to our existential angst, is a sign that our mindfulness is deepening. Whenever we are in touch with our Aliveness, angst is present. Our Consciousness comes to our attention, we notice that we exist and are unbound, and it makes us uneasy. We encounter angst as an all-too-familiar permanent condition which we've repeatedly tried to push away, ignore, and maybe even fix. In our innocence and confusion, we've gone as far as inadvertently overlooking our Beingness (most often through lots of "doing" instead of "Being") to try to avoid anxiety, and this isn't helpful. When we are radically mindful, however, we give ourselves an opening to be fearlessly present with the gloom of our malaise. "Like a baby learning to use its hands and feet, at first we only fumble around in spirit, groping in the dark until, almost by accident, we compose a posture of being that opens our spirits for existential release," writes existential philosopher James Leonard Park (2015). "Somewhere in the dark, a door opens, and we turn our spirits toward the light, hoping for another glimpse." Paradoxically, darkness, when consciously encountered, leads to light. It can serve as an entrance into a mysterious quest, a sacred moment of bittersweetness, of purgatory disillusionment, and the refreshment of not-knowing.

When we investigate our existential angst or anxiety mindfully, we find unexpected gifts—as long as we are prepared to turn within. We cannot bypass existential loneliness, however, but we can realize our oneness, universal Beingness, our seamlessly collective Consciousness—radical aloneness. As with anxiety, loneliness can be a portal to Aliveness; we just need courage, or readiness, to enter it.

It seems at first contradictory and nonsensical, but loneliness can unveil healing, love, and connection with the life that we are in all its glorious forms. Loneliness gives us space to mindfully inquire into our existential state and move with the flow. Then, whereas interpersonal loneliness is lifeless and empty, existential loneliness transmutes into fresh possibility and community, bringing authenticity and self-renewal. We must first be willing to put aside our self-centered seeking for better states and better people, to mindfully shift the focus of our attention to greater depths of existence. Then we might realize that the individual we think we are is but a foretaste of existence, and not existence itself.

Aliveness

The body-mind is a vehicle and an instrument for manifesting Aliveness—that palpable sense and knowledge of "I am" or "presence" that we know either subtly or strongly. We habitually focus Aliveness toward the mind and its contents, therefore emphasizing them and distorting our fundamental sense of "I am." Many people live from this perspective of self-consciousness, which is a localized expression of the full breadth of existence. They have no intention or inclination of looking beyond it. They may have glimpses of something expansive and beautiful—a more complete expression of Aliveness—but they quickly push away these insights because of the awe and therefore angst of such an encounter.

The immediacy of Being—your presence—accompanies you wherever you go and whatever you do, only you've inadvertently attached countless ideas and beliefs to it, all of which are inaccurate, making your Aliveness seem static and perishable. At once you exist, then through the play of imagination which gets filtered through desire and fear, you exist as "someone" or "something." Memory constructs continuity and solidity, and you end up enduring dualistic isolation along with its products of interpersonal isolation and interpersonal loneliness. As an upshot of imagining difference and contrast, you seek out "special" people to make you less lonely and "special" experiences to make you less anxious.

Aliveness itself is nothing perceivable, or imaginable, nor is it caused—it just is. To Be, and to know that one exists, is key to radical mindfulness. Just Being itself is the only assurance and the only certainty needed. Being *something* is characterized by doubt and insecurity. There's authenticity in the assertion "I am"; every other is a poor translation of Being. Nothing sticks to you. You are the Source of life, but none of your expressions capture your entirety as that Source.

Oneness

When you know that you exist as Aliveness, you might feel existentially lonely. When you know that you exist as oneness—existence itself, you are radically alone, All There Is.

You're not limited to any dualistic identity the mind can conjure. Behind your personality is the existential sense "I am" which you can't relinquish, but you can attach it to any belief. You do this verbally when you assert "I am…" statements. But such self-proclamations, however relatively useful and meaningful, are ultimately inaccurate and the cause of suffering when believed to be absolute. I think of them as creatively hinting at me but never capturing me in the same way as a single leaf (a single portion of Aliveness) is one expression of its greater whole—the oak tree (oneness). Being, Aliveness, localized consciousness, or what we could call "Life," is felt and witnessed by all because it is One; the focus of Aliveness is all that varies. Beyond differing focal points, it's the One Life that "we" are.

At first, it seems as if Aliveness is our higher identity, that we have our own share of Beingness, that there's a Being called "me" and a Being called "you." It is clearer (but not entirely accurate, as we'll discover later) to say that you are oneness—you are principally the same universal Consciousness that animates absolutely everything. And so the quality "I am" should only be used as a temporary pointer—a great pointer, but a signpost nevertheless. Poetically speaking, Consciousness has two bodies: the individual (or local) and the universal. The personal fluctuates, whereas the universal remains stable. The personal and the universal are flawlessly linked. They are expressions of the same seed.

Because you exist, all is possible. The seemingly unlimited multiverse is only a minuscule display of your inexhaustible power to be. To be a human being, however exquisite and successful in worldly terms, is not your final manifestation; you are something else beyond the limited domain of form, something unimaginably more magnificent, which isn't a *thing*.

We are what we are, already. Nevertheless, we can drop the tendency to imagine ourselves to be limited entities. The stories of our "personal self" and "universal self" are equally provisional; let us go within and beyond, and loosen our costumes even more. There's nothing to lose except an isolated phantom. When we reconcile with oneness, our universal Aliveness, we're primed to come home to Self, which is inexplicably non-dual and therefore free of anxiety, confusion, and loneliness. Please don't try to bypass your humanity, however. Recognize that you are that which *creates* and *embraces* your bittersweet humanness without condition.

CHAPTER 6

The Forest and the Trees

The message of Advaita (non-duality) is that there is only one.
There is only one presence/awareness—one being. You are that
presence/awareness—that beingness—in which the universe
and all possibilities arise. The apparent two, you and me, are
really just the one and there is nothing but that.

Everything that is, exists within what you are so it is not
separate from you. Everything is really the same thing, at best
just appearance or movement of energy expressing in countless
forms. But, creation itself is finite to the presence/awareness
that contains it.

—John Greven, *Oneness: The Destination*
You Never Left

According to Advaita Vedanta philosophy, which dates back
thousands of years, we're told of and systematically guided to
the realization that we're not defined by or limited to our personality or our body, not even to our localized consciousness;
they are purely temporary, equal expressions of supreme

reality, or the ground of existence, which Vedanta calls *Brahman*. Indefinable, Brahman is life's ultimate underlying Source, the fundamental reality, and we're invited to know this truth directly.

Our supreme Self, Brahman, illuminates our every mode of life—it's what makes existence possible. It's without a trace of duality, without a beginning or end, prior to universal laws such as cause-effect and time and space, unlimited, undivided, changeless. Calmly and silently, it permeates our every experience. It is the heart of unconditional love and joy. It's the life that you are.

The reason we don't already know our Source experientially or intellectually is due to our innocent ignorance (inadvertence, restlessness, desiring and fearing the impermanent), which is a delusional state. Experience and intellect can only take us so far. Our imagination is a symptom of the veiling power of illusion—*maya*, in Sanskrit—which gives the many expressions of Brahman, creating forms in the formlessness. Maya causes us to be preoccupied with the imagined outer world which prevents us from focusing on our inner life, which is the full breadth of life.

When we awake to our absolute Self, the dream is less convincing. The performance, however, goes on as before. Only we are no longer fooled by the roles we play or the artificial props on the stage. Loneliness and isolation were but dramatic lines within the narrative. We can, with greater lucidity, finally appreciate both "the forest and the trees," to use another metaphor.

Getting Equipped for Seeing Clearly

The Sanskrit word *yoga* (or "connection," "union") refers to a range of meditative practices intended to provide the means for rigorous attention and discrimination. Far from merely being a set of physical postures, yoga is the slowing down and eventual cessation of the activities or permutations (what I call restless inadvertence) of the body-mind. These activities appear as mental and emotional impressions, thoughts, ideas, and conceptualizing. The goal of yoga is to disentangle Consciousness from its embroilment with such changeable movement. This amplifies clarity, harmony, and balance (the quality of *sattva*) and accordingly reduces desire, distortion, fear, and aversion (the qualities of *tamas* and *rajas*). In short, yoga unites us with the absolute truth which is Self-knowledge. Once we remove the dirt from the mirror of Consciousness, we can see our true face, liberating us from the imagined external world of separateness.

One practice is Jñana yoga, yoga of wisdom or knowledge, which belongs to the Advaita Vedanta school of Hindu philosophy—*Advaita* meaning non-duality: "not two." In Jñana yoga, the mind is used as a tool for inquiry to transcend its limiting identification with the illusory world of separation. The ultimate aim is to merge with Brahman. This is achieved by earnestly practicing the techniques of focusing, self-questioning, reflection, and clarification. Philosophical pondering, introspection, and contemplation are all involved in this intensive exploration in which the mind sees the limitations of its own nature and deconstructs itself. Qualities of practice for seeking Self-knowledge or truth—the *sadhana chatushtaya* set out in Sri Adi Sankaracharya's *Crest-Jewel of Discrimination* (Madhavananda 2013)—are prescribed to the spiritual seeker, providing the steps toward liberation.

- The willingness to discriminate between the real and the unreal

- Nonattachment or dependence on the fruits of one's own actions

- The six virtues:

  1. Tranquility

  2. Restraint

  3. Withdrawal

  4. Forbearance

  5. Faith

  6. Concentration on the Self

- Intense yearning for liberation

The mindful practice of discerning what is true has Buddhist roots too, and will be an inspiration on our journey

---

* *Withdrawal—While there's no need for avoidance or abandonment, what is important in inquiry is to step back from identification with the ephemeral.*

together. One of the oldest Buddhist meditation practices is vipassana meditation, which involves examining experience to unveil its true nature (Blomfield 2012). Vipassana, meaning "to see clearly," is contemplation of the impermanent and insubstantial nature of existence.

A lot of this sounds decidedly absurd and unrealistic to the modern Western mind. But, in the lived experience of these time-honored approaches, vast wisdom and many gifts can be found. In fact, non-duality isn't unrealistic. It points beyond our deep-rooted ideas of limitation and division, embracing every expression because reality, Brahman, *is* every expression. What is unrealistic, and even nihilistic, is the belief that we're finite and limited individuals, far away from wholeness on a meaningless, frustrating, and lonely journey to an unavoidable death. The non-dual message invites us to question our life-denying selfhood wholeheartedly so that we can open up more and more to our fullness (which is also empty!). Non-dual inquiry is waking up to our completeness—our natural state.

The Natural Yoga

Sri Nisargadatta Maharaj taught what has been called Nisarga Yoga (Nisarga meaning "the natural state"), which clarifies the mind, bringing Self-awareness (1973). He didn't base his teaching on any particular theology, cosmology, psychology, or even philosophy (although it has much in common with Advaita Vedanta). He even said himself that what he was teaching might seem too simple, or even crude. Having not practiced any specific forms of meditation or spiritual practice himself, Maharaj didn't prescribe a formal spiritual method or belief system. Everyone has their own means to truth and realization, he affirmed, and there are no genuine "one-size-fits-all" techniques for Self-realization. Maharaj just lived his life and told others to do the same: "Your *sadhana*"—meaning practice—"is to be. The doing happens. Just be watchful. Where is the difficulty in remembering that you are? You are all the time" (Maharaj 1973, 236).

Following in the footsteps of his beloved guru, Sri Samartha Siddharameshwar Maharaj, Sri Nisargadatta Maharaj urged his disciples to delve into the ever-present sense of "I" to reach its Source and once and for all find lasting happiness within. Echoing the powerful instruction given to him by his teacher, he never grew tired of telling those who came to listen to him that they were not what they took themselves to be. They simply needed to find out what they were by focusing their minds on pure Being, and staying in it. "Watch the sense 'I am,'" he said over and over. "Find your real self"; "You cannot part with it, but you can impart it to anything"; "Give your heart and mind to it, think of nothing else" (Maharaj 1973, 70).

As his affectionate yet direct guidance suggests, Nisargadatta's yoga means to stay attentive to one's Beingness. This is most effective and transformative when we're attentive to Being without effort or pretense, when we naturally live meditatively and inquiringly and are familiar with shifting the focus of Consciousness. This is the continual encounter of Self-intimacy: to surrender our "small" lives to our vast lives and to let them be our teacher, to wonder earnestly, to investigate, until we arrive at the crux of the mind's misunderstanding and thus to the clarity of non-dual Knowing beyond the illusory. Then we discover that it's impossible to *be* isolated or afraid because we are everything. What is there to be scared of? Who is missing from our lives? Yes, loneliness and fear may fleetingly pass through us, and we feel them fully, but we aren't fooled into claiming them. We know the difference between superficial experience and truth. This is the utmost secure human existence; it's true friendship, harmony, and wholeness, real intimacy of Self-with-Self.

A Discerning Focus in Ordinary Life

What I have always found refreshing about the message of non-duality is that it eventually negates itself. The message, and the meditative inquiry process that it leads to, is a means and not an end; creating a non-dual person with non-dual knowledge isn't the aim. The end of separation and isolation is not cultivated as a result of special philosophy or action; it can only be lived. "Do not meditate," says Sri Ramana Maharshi, "be! Do not think that you are—be! Don't think about being—you are!" (Maharshi and Godman 1991, 57). We need not try to manufacture or maintain what is complete and eternal. Realization *is*.

In an experiential sense, we just need to clean the mirror of Deep Knowing, to blow away the dust of imagination made of particles of desire and fear. Being your absolute Self is effortless since it's always present—but familiarizing ourselves with our essential Aliveness through adopting a discerning focus will direct you toward it. In an absolute sense, the "mirror" is always clear (see *The Platform Sutra*, Red Pine, 2008).

What we are exploring is a lived mindfulness, a radical mindfulness, one that transcends formal spiritual practice. Even so and for some of us, a period of deliberate and determined formal practice (alertly and restfully sitting in silence with eyes closed, regularly, for example) often serves as a good primer. No lengthy process is necessary because Self is incontrovertible; once you get a taste for Self, it will flavor everything, just as salt imbues the entire ocean. Yes, it's possible to fine-tune the focus of localized consciousness through the technology of meditation and Self-inquiry. The essence of meditation and inquiry practice is mindfulness. When mindfulness is radical, meditation has the potential to make clear *that* we are, and inquiry can make clear *what* we are. This fusion of "that" and "what" is powerful, transformative, and illuminating. However, any insights and answers that arise, if they are truly of Self, are non-conceptual and nonverbal, yet Deeply Known nevertheless. Likewise, there's no point in holding on to the hammer once we've hit the proverbial nail on the head.

The discerning focus you'll cultivate can continue throughout daily activity in any environment and in any circumstance. This means that there's no need to give up "mundane" activities and retreat to a cave. A shift in focus doesn't mean, however, that we'll no longer face challenges. We can, nevertheless, do our best not to run away from them and to tune into a more expanded perspective—to see both the forest and the trees. Everything can become a way if we're curious, detached, earnest, and receptive.

Gradually, radical mindfulness (a shift from *mind* to *fullness*) will become increasingly subtle until it becomes a natural way of living. Undoubtedly, it is a characteristic of the mind to be very restless, so try to welcome the notion of shifting your focus beyond the mind to that which isn't caught up in distorted superficiality. If you're curious, you've already made a significant leap of consciousness!

Before the rise of formal education, the apprentice pursuing a traditional craft would first study the basics of how to use the tools and materials applicable to his craft. To this end, immense practice was crucial for mastering the fundamentals. In the course of learning, the craftsperson would over time conceive a personal style and approach and at some point become a master craftsperson, with the cumulative creation of a masterpiece.

SEER CRAFTS for Radical Mindfulness

What follows is a map for radical mindfulness comprising a group of qualities and skills related to discerning focus, which we'll explore in depth throughout the next ten chapters. Since mindfulness clarifies our experience, the four qualities involved are arranged by an acronym that you can use as a mnemonic, SEER, while the mnemonic CRAFTS sets out the six skills involved. So, radical mindfulness is the art of seeing—coming to know ourselves as the ultimate seer, the Self, the unimaginable fullness and emptiness of life that we are.

When I use the word "seeing," I'm not referring to the gross capacity of sight as associated with the organ of the eyes or even the visual imagining of the mind. I'm using the notion in an entirely different way, as an allegory for Awareness itself, which "sees" in the sense of recognizing Aliveness in everything and everything in Aliveness. Whereas our physical eyes and mind might perceive a tree and a house set within a scene of otherness and density, our spiritual eyes of Awareness see all objects as a single transitory display of energetic Aliveness which itself is a manifestation of timeless Awareness.

Through the SEER CRAFTS, we (or more specifically, the body-mind) gradually stop misidentifying the Self with the body-mind's shortsighted perception and therefore stop believing the Self to be subject to birth and death, desire and fear. As we're discovering, this innocent misidentification is a by-product of separateness, and is the root of bondage and suffering. The way to liberation (of course, we're never truly held captive) is earnest, meditative discernment. You can develop this discernment by cultivating the skills below.

The SEER Qualities

- **S**incere curiosity: An openness to exploring life with fresh eyes and an open heart

- **E**mbracing and releasing experience: Honoring what is present, knowing it will pass

- **E**arnest questioning: Deeply investigating assumptions and ideas about ourselves, others, and life

- **R**eceptiveness to truth: Getting out of the way and allowing the "bigger picture" to present itself

The Radically Mindful CRAFTS

- **C**ourage: The readiness and fortitude to inquire, not being led astray by fear or the need for comfort

- **R**emembrance of Self: Reconnecting with the most authentic version of ourselves

- **A**ttention: Knowing that the art of living is a matter of focus

- **F**ullness and emptiness: Holding everything and nothing in balance

- **T**ranquility: Tapping into the still, silent place beneath the restlessness of the mind

- **S**urrender: Making peace with what is, not trying to reach a final conclusion or ideal

It's worth mentioning again that this framework is designed to be descriptive and not prescriptive. I am not advocating a particular practice, but offering the principles, qualities, and skills which I (and many others) have found to be invaluable in my own search for truth. The ordering of the above isn't all that important. Or more exactly, if the SEER CRAFTS were a sandwich, "Sincere curiosity" and "Surrender" would be the bread providing a foundation; the other qualities and skills would be the sandwich filling, and as such, they could be positioned in any order. In other words, what matters is that we remember that radical mindfulness begins with curiosity and ends with surrender. We'll explore the first SEER quality in the next chapter.

Remember that each of the SEER CRAFTS has a musical representation which you can listen to while reading, reflecting, inquiring, relaxing, or meditating. Think of these as your radically mindful "soundtrack" to living the life that you are. Go to http://www.newharbinger.com/40859 to access these tracks.

CHAPTER 7

The First SEER Quality: Sincere Curiosity

The Self which is free from sin, free from old age, from death and grief, from hunger and thirst, which desires nothing but what it ought to desire, and imagines nothing but what it ought to imagine, that it is which we must search out, that it is which we must try to understand.

—*Chandogya Upanishad 8.7.1*

Curiosity is key to radical mindfulness. It is the heart of discerning focus and the opposite of the mind's default state of restless inadvertence. At this point in our journey, just let your curiosity blossom and open like a flower bud. A gentle inquisitiveness about the present will soften your stories about the past and future, making space for expansive potential. For example, witnessing your mind's disposition to jump to conclusions and its desire to seek answers can help you become

Go to http://www.newharbinger.com/40859 to listen to "Sincere Curiosity."

more open; and it's this open span of Consciousness that is required to be awake to truth.

What were you curious about as a child? What are you curious about now?

Remember a time when you were experiencing something with wonder. Before the mind started analyzing or naming, you must have been in a state of pure openness, receptive to genuine understanding. When we wonder, real inquiry can begin. In wondering, we witness the answers that come and go and stay receptive to deeper nonintellectual insight. More exactly, we can sense the wonder in the fact that we exist, that as focal points of Aliveness we can be awake to life. If we really look beyond the knowledge we have accumulated, we can find wonder in absolutely everything. You can look now.

Loosen Up

Inquire: Can we capture the exact meaning of anything with words and thoughts? Is that possible? Does anything have any inherent, ultimate meaning? Are definitions the same as truth? Can truth be defined? Can you be defined?

Definitions are inherited: secondhand labels, innocent attempts to capture and quantify life. This capturing gives way to the belief in limitation and separation, and primarily, suffering. We feel secure as a something—as an anything— but it's a conditional and unstable pseudo-security. Through our avoidance of vulnerability, we've lost a lot of our curiosity about existing. So much of our suffering is due to our safety labeling, which creates an oppressive and fearful experience of life.

Of course, ascribing meaning loosely and playfully can be practical. But as soon as we are convinced that the meanings and definitions are set in stone and definitive, we become lost in the dream of our own storytelling. We take refuge in purpose and meaning. The mind is a meaning-making machine. Stories based on fabricated meaning are created and reinforced by thought, and little evidence is required for these flimsy narratives to disguise themselves as substantial and compelling truths. Meaning is not the same as truth.

There is abundant joy, and freedom too, in not-knowing and not needing to know. These are the same joy and freedom that have been obscured by our grasping onto concepts. When our ideas and conclusions dissolve, we can rediscover clarity. Releasing the assumptions built into our existential questions is infinitely more illuminating than gaining secondhand answers. Curiosity is the antidote to the static limitations of certainty, inevitability, and solidity. A curious outlook is brimming with spontaneous Aliveness. Cerebral answers are dead and cold. So loosen up! There's nothing complacent or ignorant with beginning and ending with the wise thought, "I don't know." Quite the reverse is true; admitting we can't know anything for sure means taking an honest stance of open-ended inquiry into your experience. As *A Course in*

Miracles teaches us, "questioning illusions is the first step in undoing them" (Foundation for Inner Peace 2007).

Sri Nisargadatta Maharaj described himself as having the curiosity of a child, but his wasn't a curiosity that made him feel insecure and hanker for refuge in worldly knowledge (1973). In contrast, his security was in Self-knowledge, which is freedom from the separate self and its unstable world. He taught that as we embrace dispassion and detachment, we lose interest in the knowledge-based dream of duality and stimulate our interest in the truth beyond imagination. Then, curiosity becomes earnestness, zeal, and trust in one's heart.

As a child, did you ever scoop sand in your hands? What happened when you held it tightly in your grip? Held gently, with an open hand, the sand stays where it is. The moment we close our hand and squeeze firmly, the sand seeps through our fingers. We may grasp it, but nearly all of it will be lost.

Not-Knowing

Not-knowing is fertile ground, not a barren wasteland. Before we can discover anything fresh and new, we need to rest into a relaxed but attentive state of not-knowing. This may be obvious, but if we're honest, we're not very comfortable with not-knowing, are we? Avoiding the apparent ignorance and ambiguity of not-knowing, we instead look for confirmation of what we believe we are sure of, therefore defeating the purpose of inquiry. At the same time, avoiding ambiguity has a function. Not-knowing is death to the mind, and death is the most extreme and final form of not-knowing.

But not-knowing, in spiritual practice, isn't necessarily the absence of knowledge; it's a natural foundation on which knowledge comes and fades away. Spiritual maturity involves an uncensored letting go, not a perpetual amassing. You don't even need to let go. You *are* the natural release.

We know nothing; not really, anyway—just a bunch of inherited stories. When we confess this, when we stop projecting our (necessarily) limited knowledge out to the world, then we just *know*. The only authority is this moment. This is the end of control and hope to the mind. We're not the mind; we are the Aliveness of this moment, so this isn't resignation or passivity. It's realizing not-knowing, which is the only way to encounter life authentically and to inquire into it.

Is any concept, belief, or idea absolute? The mind thinks in absolute ways about the relative, causing the relative to masquerade as the absolute and the absolute the relative. A world of relatives (or duality) has no true absolutes. The mind-made separate self detests not-knowing; it desires more certainty and fears the loss of certainty. How does not-knowing make you feel? While asking yourself this question, notice how your mind spins time-based stories to move away from this apparently ambiguous moment. Here's another question: Is anything actually certain? We may feel anxious at first when we ask this question (anxiety's okay, remember), and this is why we need readiness and willingness—courage.

When our sincere curiosity rises, and our expectations fade, we can live life as it is with equanimity. We become alerted to fascinating subtleties and discover an effortless fulfillment that is unqualified and forever present. This moment, which is bursting with raw wonder and richness, holds all the authentic responses to our inquiry.

CHAPTER 8

The Second SEER Quality: Embracing and Releasing Experience

He is the one God, hidden in all beings, all-pervading, the self within all beings, watching over all works, dwelling in all beings, the witness, the perceiver, the only one, free from qualities.

—Svetâsvatara Upanishad 6.11

What's your present experience? Who's the experiencer? What observes both the experience and the experiencer? What is aware of the observer?

We usually search for what we most deeply desire within the impermanent appearances of life: within thoughts, states, feelings, self-concepts, and other people. If we can reinforce

Go to http://www.newharbinger.com/40859 to listen to "Embracing and Releasing Experience."

this stuff, we think, everything will work out well. But in reality, these things simply can't bring true fulfillment because they're incapable of fully encapsulating life. Notice how such grasping is unsatisfactory because what we cling to doesn't last, and what doesn't last can't bring lasting happiness. Metaphorically speaking, we cannot keep hold of appearances any more than we can grasp sand. In fact, our experience is an unceasing flow of phenomena; it unfolds and dissolves in our Beingness—the distinct feeling and Deep Knowing of our permeating actuality.

We seek to manifest what we desire by avoiding, removing, or moving away from the things that don't match what we're pursuing. While it's a creative strategy of the mind, our impatient and insatiable quests won't bring us what we want— they'll only create more unease. Through restless inadvertence, we've forgotten our abiding Self and through embracing—and releasing—experience, we can find it again. When we do, the mind can leave the manifesting in the hands of our Self, because it has a much better Awareness of reality than the mind ever will.

Contrasting Yet Complementary

To illustrate the releasing and embracing I'm describing, bring to mind the yin-yang symbol. In Taoist philosophy, the yin-yang symbol represents the connectedness and relatedness of contrary forces (Yao 2010). Yin embraces yang and yang embraces yin, and contained within each is a piece of the other. These forces both create and neutralize each other, and they're held without condition within the completeness of the encompassing circle, or Awareness. The symbol shows how each piece has a rightful place: dark and light, male and female, and how when we focus on one or the other, a segment of that energy is ignored. But when we hold both, however difficult, we expose fresh insight and wisdom.

While its contrasting contents are always in a restless state of flux, the circle—which holds the two forces—remains the same, unblemished and complete. The circle offers a background onto which disparate phenomena are projected and held. Without this essential screen, the wonderful display of life we experience wouldn't appear.

The symbolic circle which holds yin-yang can represent the eternal "holding" presence, our permeating Aliveness. Whatever is present—thoughts, emotions, mental images, sensations, smells, tastes, and the objects these sensory building blocks fashion—is life itself. What is here right now is contained by, complete within, and born of what you are. This is a containment without limits: no walls, doors, bricks, gates, or roofs. No boundaries. No isolation. Despite appearances, everything holds the key to the "Gateless Gate," as Wumen Hui-k'ai called it (Sekida 2005); knowing how to use the key is what's needed.

Yin and yang complement one another. In the same way, the purpose of radical mindfulness isn't to eradicate duality. The purpose is to recognize that duality, or the appearance of separation, has an unconditional place within life, or undivided wholeness. The eradication of duality—if it were at all achievable—might cause a pure state of oneness, but this is still another extreme. Indeed, the concept of oneness would instantly perish without its counterpart "duality." Both are provisional concepts, and we should use them as such.

Yes, there most certainly seems to be an appearance of duality, contrast, and distinction, of fragmentation. Take a look at all the disparate objects around yourself right now. See how the mind automatically labels each thing. See the memories and associations that are triggered by each object. But ask: Are the objects the labels and associations? Aren't the labels just inherited stories? Can you know or say what any of this stuff is?

Appearance Is Acceptance

What's appearing for you right now in your inner and outer scope of Awareness?

Which appearances are acceptable to you? Which appearances are unacceptable to you? What are your fears about the unacceptable things? What are your desires about the unacceptable things? What are your fears about the acceptable things? What are your desires about the acceptable things? Are your desires and fears absolutely justified?

Now consider this: Appearance is acceptance. Sit with this notion for a while: beyond the mind's judgmental narrative, appearance is acceptance.

Life through human eyes is bittersweet. We experience the rough with the smooth, the light with the dark, the gain with the loss, the agony with the ecstasy. The opposites naturally create and depend on each other. But because we often experience ourselves as separate, we pursue one side of the existential coin and flee or try to deny the other. But it doesn't work. The truth is that we are life in its entirety, but in not recognizing this we leave out parts of ourselves—we endeavor to achieve inclusion via exclusion.

Is our inquiry about trying to accept our many manifestations? No trying is required. The point is that life freely accepts and has boundless capacity for "existential holding". It's always present. It's your Aliveness. Just be conscious of your natural flow with the "isness"—that's all. You are both the "happening" and the "flow"—they're inseparable. Stop trying to accept and *be* the acceptance.

Bring your attention to the effortless quality of "holding." Glance around at everything in your scope of experience (internal and external): sights, sounds, smells, tastes, textures, thoughts, feelings, as well as your identities and your vital Aliveness. Try to comprehend experientially that whatever is unfolding in your present experience has full permission to appear in and as you. Welcome the notion that all of this is temporary. Nothing is final. Ask: "What knows the contents of this capacity deeply?"; "From where does this holding capacity arise?"

As Being Aliveness, we already allow this whole play of twoness, distinction, and contrast—even our sense of loneliness and isolation. No one need do the accepting; the fact of the appearance or existence of something *is* the accepting. Imagine a table on which there are various objects. Despite the apparent beauty, ugliness, or neutrality of the objects, all are held equally by the table. Within the very presence of something is its inherent nonresistance.

Love is both the rediscovery of inseparability and the radical acceptance of duality. Love is forever recognizing itself. *Loving* the life that we are is *living* the life that we are. *Living* the life that we are is *loving* the life that we are.

CHAPTER 9

The Third SEER Quality: Earnest Questioning

The real is gained by Wisdom, not by a myriad of rites. When one steadily examines and clearly sees a rope, the fear that it is a serpent is destroyed. Knowledge is gained by discernment, by examining, by instruction, but not by bathing, nor gifts, nor a hundred holdings of the breath.

—Adi Shankara, *Vivekachudamani* v12

We desire meaning and fear disorder. We want to live in an orderly world that we can understand. We want everything to be tied up neatly with a pretty bow, as if we have a compulsive need to order and control everything around us. The impact of this is that we're always trying to comprehend how to position ourselves and how to be. When we're outsiders trying to get into a contradictory world that refuses to meet our desires,

Go to http://www.newharbinger.com/40859 to listen to "Earnest Questioning."

we start to feel existentially anxious. We might start asking big questions like "Who am I?" Far from being a disaster or something to fear, this is the start of radically mindful inquiry which calls for courage and earnest questioning. To be earnest, we have to be radically authentic, flexible, open, and honest.

Who Am I?

The question "Who am I?" is a tool which helps us move our focus from objects of localized consciousness to the ultimate holder of them. Self-inquiry is not psychological analysis or problem solving, because life isn't a problem to be solved; it's an ever-fresh interaction we immerse ourselves in and stay in receptively and wakefully. In this way, we ask "Who am I?" with a different outlook from that of psychology or other schools of thought. Intellectual answers are not the target. In other words, we're not speculating or dreaming up explanations (not to say that this doesn't have its place); inquiry, in contrast, is direct observation and complete openness.

In an ontological sense, "Who am I?" means "What is the nature of my Aliveness in the universal sense?", "What is it to exist?", and "What is at the heart of existence?" These questions start from the position that Life is a single happening. There is, therefore, a kind of radical aloneness in asking this question, but it takes us closer toward that which is free of any implied duality. In earnestly examining our experience, our focus widens, which allows us to stay receptive and awake to truth.

Become silent, supple, and soft. Ask the question: "Am I limited and restricted to being human?" There's no need to answer; simply note any response and do nothing with it. Ask: "What is conscious of this response?" and "What is the Beingness in being human?" Focus on that sense of simple Being, however subtle or strong. See if you can recognize it as the presence that has been with you every moment of your entire life. Inquire: "From where does this Being emerge?" Remain receptive and quiet and rest into your focusing for a few more minutes. Let Awareness emerge; that is, Know Deeply. You might witness how the mind's habits— the play of thoughts, feelings, memories, and fantasies—try to overwhelm this restful quality of pure openness. Don't fight it. Welcome all that visits your mindfulness. When thoughts come into focus, ask: "Who knows these thoughts?" Step back and just notice.

The above exercise is influenced by three powerful Self-inquiry questions prescribed by Sri Ramana Maharshi (Thorne 2005), which I'll list below for clarity:

1. "Who am I?"

2. "Who knows these thoughts?"

3. "From where has this I arisen?"

As with Nisarga Yoga (see chapter 6), the purpose of Ramana Maharshi's method is to stabilize focus in our natural presence of Being. These questions give us the power of lucid discernment which illuminates the real.

Discernment Through Negation

Mindful negation (or the Vedic *neti-neti*, which translates to "Not this, not this") gives us a refreshing alternative to the automatic habit of self-limitation which is Self-denial. It broadens our scope of focus by guiding us in our observation of our concepts and systematically seeing through them.

As Sri Nisargadatta Maharaj said, to know what we are, we must first find out what we are not (1973). We aren't a story the mind can perceive or conceive because the mind can only imagine. More specifically, because we can and do most beautifully express ourselves in countless ways, it's clearer to say that we aren't *limited* to our self-imaginings, however miraculously creative they are.

Ask yourself if your self-beliefs can capture your fullness. Are you limited to your self-definitions, or are they actually just finite expressions of your infinity? For example, "Am I male?" No, this label doesn't capture all that I am. "Am I my age?" No, that's just a number. "Am I my name?" No, that was given to me. "Am I this body?" No, my consciousness seems to transcend this flesh and these bones. "Do I have a consciousness?" No, not even consciousness defines me; it's just a word with associated mental imagery. "From whence does consciousness emerge?" I don't know, and that not-knowing feels liberating. "Where does the real me reside?" Here, there, everywhere, and nowhere.

Mindful negation dissolves the seemingly fixed roles we've attributed to ourselves and others, allowing us to appreciate our shared radical aloneness, which isn't aloneness in the usual sense but the undeniable singular Source that we are. It's the truth that speaks for itself when make-believe certainty is seen to be subjective and insubstantial.

Earnestness

The most important quality on the circular path of inquiry is earnestness. Being earnest means relating to life (ourselves) attentively and mindfully, from a stance of questioning with focus and discernment. Once we walk through the veil of untruths we've created out of restless inadvertence, we can love what is without expectation. Experientially, we live in tune with our Self as an infinite possibility and discover a deeper realization and joy that the mind could never muster.

In inquiry, we don't question to get hold of answers but to release our assumptions. We inquire (and meditate) to extend our focus of consciousness and to welcome that which we can't capture with words or thought. Therein lies genuine peace, understanding, and contentment. Because, after all, this unquantifiable no-thing is the "answer" we most desire, not the half-baked, contradictory hand-me-downs we're accustomed to. Beyond knowledge and its definable world, you know this. When, through being earnest, this fact hits home experientially, and we realize that conclusions are just sticking Band-Aids, we find a way of living with the reality that no valid answers will be forthcoming. There's a surprising equanimity in this. We stop trying to impose conceptual boundaries, and life's fullness shines more brightly—a fullness which transcends and exists before the mind.

Living the life that we are with radical mindfulness doesn't end in reaching a final destination, so even the "truth" signpost is temporary. Indeed, our motionless journey is to rediscover our origin and root ourselves in wholeness which is here and now. On an experiential level, this is authentic living.

CHAPTER 10

The Fourth SEER Quality: Receptiveness to Truth

That immortal Brahman is before, that Brahman is behind, that Brahman is right and left. It has gone forth below and above; Brahman alone is all this, it is the best.

—*Mundaka Upanishad 2.2.11*

A plant's striking ability to sense and move toward the light is crucial for its growth and existence. Through light receptors, plants are able to differentiate and develop in response to light, allowing them to enhance their use of light and space (Lumen Learning 2016). Like a light-seeking plant, many people since ancient times have practiced meditation as a way of being receptive to truth: of becoming familiar with and rooted in their most authentic Self.

Go to http://www.newharbinger.com/40859 to listen to "Receptiveness to Truth."

Receptivity

Meditation, to me, is a tool for recognizing clearly; with practice, falsehoods and distractions are cast off, and then with earnestness and devotion one focuses on what remains, thus becoming awake to truth. Meditation has been mystified, commercialized, and commodified. In truth, meditation is the simple act of watching wherefrom Aliveness originates, therefore absorbing the body and mind in that nameless no-thing that remains. It's the practice of mindfulness: being alert to what's going on in the present moment with lucidity and gentleness. In doing so, we can witness with clarity both "the forest and the trees"—a varifocal insight, if you will. If truth be told, we can do this on and off the meditation mat.

Even amid everyday activity, we can find that this receptivity is happening under the surface of the mind and is readily available. We need to create space in the restless stream of thought to access it. We do this by observing it and returning again and again to our focus of localized consciousness. This helps us appreciate that fleeting phenomena—thoughts, emotions, sensations, and mental images—arise from Awareness (which I call Deep Knowing) and fall back into Awareness, and that knowing, albeit frequently obscured, is undeviating. Ordinary existence continues, but we are in touch with our most loyal companion—our Aliveness—which connects us to our original home.

Meditation is a way of living, not just a practice we sometimes do. It isn't a strategy, a way to escape, a quick fix, or even a technique for self-improvement. Conversely, meditation is an uncensored embrace of our present experience with courage, letting life unfold as it will, but not getting enmeshed in and identifying with that unfolding. This loving, existential embrace reveals the way to healing, to deeper understanding, to authentic unity with the universal. Suffering, if held and assimilated into universal Consciousness and no longer escaped and shunned, teaches us to be even more sensitive and receptive to contented possibilities of truth.

Truth

The SEER qualities of Sincere curiosity, Embracing and releasing experience, and Earnest questioning feed our Receptiveness to reality, and experiential freedom is the gift of truth. The intense yearning for liberation you feel results from catching sight of your tendency to get trapped in the cycle of restless inadvertence. Do you see the futility of this automatic mechanism? By being receptive, you can stop investing your energy in it and be open to reaching outside it, like a plant feeling its way through obscurity. Sri Sankaracharya referred to *mumukshuta* as the wish to free oneself from false identifications by realizing truth. This is a deep urge, an earnestness for one's fullness, an inclination to know the actuality of existence, a desire which intuits something else beyond body-mind desire (Swami Madhavananda 1921).

Receptiveness to truth is a direct and expansive seeing of life, a "whole-seeing" or "in-seeing," which is entirely different from intellectual perceiving (Balsekar 1982). It is knowing deeply, intuitively that what we are is the inexhaustible animating force which births the world of multiplicity, but, and most importantly, the total freedom amid multiplicity. We are beyond both Being and non-Being. No other guide is needed but to let this basic but expansive recognition impregnate our localized consciousness. As long as our longing for truth affects our daily lives, Maharaj reassures us, all is well.

Anytime it's articulated instead of directly recognized and Deeply Known, truth becomes a concept. As soon as we talk about truth, our very conceptualizing distorts it! As I said in the previous chapter, truth speaks for itself when we attend to falsehood (including ideas about truth!). An important hint is that whereas the unreal is impermanent and relative, truth is permanent and absolute. Truth—the *infinite*—has no opposite at all; it doesn't appear in degrees or shades because it's absolutely all-inclusive. Being all-inclusive, the infinite is not opposed to the finite. All the forms you're witnessing right now are proof of this. Appearance, however, being limited, cannot encompass truth, only hint at it. Awareness of form is acceptance of form. Therefore, everything is a portal into the boundless heart of life. When the seer in us wakes up and becomes receptive, we stop taking things for granted or at face value—we're primed for truth.

Annamalai Swami, a direct student of Ramana Maharshi, pointed to this in his own talks. He said that we should keep this truth in mind at all times, not allowing ourselves to be fooled into believing that anything else (such as limited identifications) is real (Annamalai and Godman 2000). Annamalai distinguished between the mind and the Self, emphasizing that it's not the Self that needs to stabilize itself, but the habitually agitated, inattentive mind. If we recognize the falsity of duality, the all-inclusive-all-exclusive Self alone remains, and we know ourselves to be that Self. In this *sadhana*, or practice, we are flowing back to the Source from which we came, just as a river naturally finds its way to the ocean. Human consciousness—so often experienced as existential aloneness—needs the river of universal Consciousness, of radical aloneness, to move it back to its infinite body. Annamalai did not advise allocated periods of meditating with one's eyes closed, because this seeing through the false and flowing with and being attentive to the Self is a living sadhana, a natural yoga—radical mindfulness. It's enough that we are persistently receptive to our Self, he said, and that we return frequently to Self-remembrance until the one who remembers and the remembered merge.

Over the next few days, try to give attention to contradictions, paradoxes, and inconsistencies, and contemplate the notion that they're a subtle yet eye-opening disclosure of truth. They are the holes in the ensnaring net. They are the gaps in the mystifying cloud. Be mindful of how all the conceptual opposites appear in the same space: the sacred and the worldly, the joy and the sadness, the vulture and the hummingbird, the agony and the bliss, the flower and seemingly vulgar things. Watch all "your" identity patterns coming and going, some light and others dark.

Do any of them successfully capture the truth about you? Notice how the apparent opposites cancel each other out by their shared presence! Then what's left? Witness how the dualities of life both create and dilute each other and are embraced within the same completeness. Life is a non-dual celebration of duality.

CHAPTER 11

The First CRAFT Skill: Courage

*Lead me from the unreal to the real! Lead me from darkness
to light! Lead me from death to immortality!*

—*Brihadâranyaka Upanishad* 1.3.28

"Existential angst" is a term coined by existential philosophers. I see it as an all-pervading anxiety that comes at us
from everywhere and nowhere. It's not the same as our fight-
flight-freeze response, which is necessary for survival and
comes and goes depending on conditions of psychological and
physical security. Unlike fear, existential angst comes and
stays because it has nothing to do with security and everything to do with freedom. What the experience of fear and
anxiety do have in common, however, is that they're both a
common response to encountering truth. Yet our minds are
comfortable within conceptual confines, in the cozy little
room of limitation. The prospect of freedom is daunting to

Go to http://www.newharbinger.com/40859 to listen to "Courage."

them. But as Aliveness itself, we are always free—however threatening that may seem. Courage is the most authentic and creative response to the anxiety that comes with living: to face the fact of our existence and to become naturally intimate and familiar with it. In the words of Nisargadatta Maharaj: "We find it difficult to be alone without any activity. It means it is not easy to tolerate our consciousness. Different types of entertainment are designed to enable us to escape from ourselves." It is courageous to remain alone and face ourselves, Maharaj continues, and in doing so we become one with Self (Gaitonde 2017).

Without courage and the type of mindfulness we're exploring, it's difficult to discern the difference between fear—a response to things in the world that frighten us—and the existential anxiety which is a pervasive non-psychological "terror" caused by nothing but our existence. Believing fear and anxiety to be the same, we inadvertently try to apply the same fixes to both. One of these fixes is relationships. Relationships can temporarily solve our *interpersonal* loneliness and isolation. They can give solidarity and unity and therefore reinforce a collective identity and security. But they can't physically merge our separate bodies and minds, as our love songs promise. And they can't resolve our *existential* loneliness and isolation, which are manifestations of our existential malaise. Put another way, relationships may superficially distract us from our free-floating unease, but they cannot free us from it. Though they might obscure it, relationships don't resolve our dualistic isolation. But facing anxiety with courage and without distraction or projection discloses the depth of Aliveness, our abundant aloneness. In doing so, we no longer use others to feel existentially secure. When we live without being compelled by ideas of being separate, we are freed to relate from a heart of fullness rather than ego-based scarcity, therefore freeing the "other." Freedom makes itself known when we don't crave anything. Courageously, we make peace with ourselves and those in our lives, a most extraordinary gift that comes from surrendering our addiction to the deficient self.

Facing the Fact of Our Existence

In the words of Paul Tillich, the Christian existentialist philosopher and theologian, we must find the "courage to be" (2014), for having courage is affirming the life that we are. Then, when an existential crisis is wholeheartedly met, understood, and surrendered to, loneliness is not a gap to be filled in but a bridge to truth. In the same way, anxiety uncovers the breathtaking reality of what we are. Anxiety reveals to us our Aliveness as the ultimate guide.

What matters is our willingness to be honest about our experience—what we're sitting with, including resistance and wanting to escape, says my friend Fiona Robertson (2017), a senior facilitator and trainer of The Living Inquiries. Any resistance and desire to get away *is* this anxiety I'm describing. An open mind and a degree of willingness are crucial because they make us ready and receptive "to investigate the truth of what we've believed for so long and start to question the basic assumptions that have underpinned our story of deficiency: that there is a solid, separate 'me'; that there is something wrong with 'me'; that steps are needed to be taken to improve 'me'; that there is a destination to reach in order for 'me' to be okay." Fiona has spent many hours with her clients, closely examining evidence that backs up their beliefs. The evidence is in the form of stories such as: "I don't belong," "I can't commit," "I shouldn't need," "I'm not enlightened," "I'm not good enough," and "I'm insatiably needy." What becomes clear with the willingness to inquire is that the objects that once were taken as proof of separation and deficiency simply can't possibly be taken as proof of anything. "The identity that we've believed in so completely begins to fall apart as the flimsy, insubstantial nature of the evidence is revealed…none of it adds up to a coherent whole," says Fiona. "Every time we take a look, more is revealed, and yet we find less. The less we find, the fuller life gets. This is truly paradoxical and absolutely breathtaking" (Robertson 2017, 31).

You Are Courageous Because You Exist

Because it's free and non-conceptual, life fearlessly holds the pseudo-existence of every impermanent and limited life-form—life has boundless capacity and affection for any expression. Conversely, a divided part lacks the power to embrace the whole, just as a wave shares the presence of the ocean but can never independently encompass it. Nevertheless, as figurative waves, we need to be willing to reach beyond the separate individual to release our anxiety and loneliness, but this is only a play of perspective.

The ego is transcendent, said Jean-Paul Sartre (2004). You can notice this for yourself right now as you read. When you're absorbed in an activity such as reading a book, Sartre observed, there is localized consciousness of the book, of its narrative, but the sense of self doesn't occupy this consciousness. Consciousness is absorbed in reading, and there is no ego. Sartre wondered if the role of the ego was to conceal from consciousness its own spontaneity so as to avoid anxiety, because its spontaneous nature, which is beyond even freedom, was the cause of anxiety. Courage, from a radically mindful perspective, is a willingness to watch our ego masks drop away and be rooted in the tender fearlessness and sanctuary of our Self.

Are you a wave (ego, small self) or the ocean (Aliveness), or perhaps both of these expressions simultaneously? If, in truth, you are basically water and water is all there is, can you truthfully conclude and claim such oneness, for doesn't the concept "oneness" suggest another subtle layer of duality and isolation? What I am saying here is that you are beyond even the "ocean." You are the supreme non-dual Self, the Ultimate Source of the vast ocean, and even these labels can be seen as provisional for they point past personality. Freedom is found in Being and having less, not more.

If we embrace our angst and look at it rather than trying to escape, analyze, or medicate it, we give ourselves the unexpected gift of a gentle Self-intimacy. We discover Self-compassion and fresh insights therein. If we find the courage or readiness to enter into this condition fully, it becomes a catalyst for Self-realization. Anxiety and loneliness can be routes back to Self. No one else can walk them except us, and there's no other time to walk them except now. Through earnest questioning and receptivity, we awaken to infinite possibility.

CHAPTER 12

The Second CRAFT Skill: Remembrance of Self

He who has his mind Self-absorbed in union, seeing the same everywhere, sees the Self in all beings and all beings in the Self.

—Bhagavad Gita 6.29

Mystified by our very presence, and without the clarity of path or purpose, we are a civilization with amnesia lost to the miracle of our own Aliveness. We're forgetful and inattentive. In their current state, our minds are too limited to fathom the boundlessness of life, too regulated by fear to enjoy the blessings of abundance freely given. Though they're miraculous in their own right, our minds are too noisy to heed the learnings in silence. They're invariably too agitated to sense the tranquility inherent within every life-born form, and too desirous to rest into the hands of love open to us.

Go to http://www.newharbinger.com/40859 to listen to "Remembrance of Self."

Sometimes when feeling helpless and alone, we shine our flashlight into the murky darkness trying to search for other lights, and yet do not wonder about the abundant Source of the light we emit—the light and life that we are already. If we do wonder, we might begin to feel anxious as we encounter our Aliveness and this angst can be disturbing, as we explored earlier. It feels comfortable, if only on a superficial level, to stay in ignorance and confusion.

The Ultimate Fear, the Final Desire

The ultimate object of our fear is the extinction (or blotting out, or death) of our body-mind. Every fear holds the dread of bodily death. Hiding within our response to everyday threats (both physical and psychological, big or small) is the disquieting unconscious dread of extinction. For instance, even the panic we experience before giving a speech to a large audience can be life-threatening; our bodies prepare for the worst whether there's an actual danger or not. Because our bodies and minds are limited, they are always in a state of vulnerability; they need protection. If we're forgetful of Self and instead identify with our fragile biological shells, we're bound to experience many shades of isolation.

Now, it sounds contradictory, but not only do we fear to lose our shell, we also desire to transcend it. Every desire aims to heighten and deepen our sense of existence. You desired a body because you wanted to experience being alive. But now you're waking up to the fact that this human manifestation limits your entirety as Life and this is a painful quandary.

The main way we try to transcend the shell is through our relationship with others. We want to belong to something bigger than what we take ourselves to be, so we imagine otherness. Because we're unsure about who we are, we try to find security and answers beyond ourselves. Through our emotional connections, we desire acceptance, approval, recognition, and to be valued for who we are. Of course, though relationships are not the solution, as long as they're healthy, stable, and resilient, they can ease our fleeting insecurities. Some even seem to bring us closer to what we seek—the home of our unmasked Self. But what remains subtly terrifying is that relationships can't help us escape death. Our intentions in pursuing them are sound because we have an inkling that our shell is insubstantial and nonrepresentative of our true identity. Our focus, however, in turning to relationships, is narrow and misguided because there are no others! We're chasing phantoms. There's only the light of our own Aliveness. We are one, radically alone, and we can find the courage to gaze into the mighty all-consuming fire of Aliveness. Only the false will burn, and only the truth will remain.

A knowing mind steps back and watches the currents of desire and fear ebb and flow while not getting caught up in the restlessness they evoke. There will be a sensation of something that is witnessing even the witnessing mind. Go with that—you're on the way to oneness.

Self-intimacy is true connection. In this sacred remembering, we find authentic acceptance, approval, recognition, and validation, which our desire-and-fear-based relationships could ever only promise. So, when you're lost, isolated, and afraid, it's not because there's a link missing in your life; it's because you're unknowingly overlooking the fundamental truth that you are this ultimate link, the common factor, pure connectivity itself.

Being Is the Great Reminder

As a child, when out shopping in the city with my mother, we'd often walk past a group of funny-looking people dressed in orange gowns and with shaved heads, happily singing a strange repetitive song. Occasionally I heard fellow shoppers moan "Oh, the bloody Harry Krishners are back" as they crossed over the road to avoid them. Although their song sounded pretty pointless and nonsensical to me at the time, there was something intensely beautiful and compelling about it. I didn't realize that their Great Mantra "Hare, Krishna, Rama" was composed of three Sanskrit names of supreme Being, that the group was devotedly calling me back to myself. They were saying over and over, "You know that you are, don't you? You know that you exist? Remember the Self that you are."

Take a deep, deliberate breath. Notice that you're breathing. In a way, you're being breathed. Watch how the air enters and leaves your body. Listen to the sound of your exhaling and inhaling, almost as if a wordless mantra (or "japa") is being recited. You're simply listening in and using it as a "metronome" to keep you focused on your essential Beingness. You may experience it as a feeling, a knowing, a resonance, or even a view of your permeating Aliveness. Check into your body and notice that you're alive. You might even say the words "I am" several times. Don't analyze or try to quantify this sense of Aliveness; just observe it and feel it. Feel the raw life energy vibrating throughout your senses, calling out to you with whispers of tenderness; dancing, pulsating, whirling with sobering joy. Aren't you aware, perhaps subtlety or strongly, of a life-giving force moving through you and animating your presence? Contemplate where this energy arises from and let go of any intellectual answers which materialize.

All you had to do to reestablish this connection to Self was to remember to be and to be mindful of your Beingness (Aliveness). This, therefore, is not a doing, but a natural encountering. It's a Self-intimacy which reveals what you always are beyond description, a homecoming unfolding in radical aloneness. Once you get accustomed to reestablishing this connection, without desiring or fearing being this or that, you'll find it amid daily experiences quite spontaneously. You'll be increasingly less likely to be misled by the mind's commotion. Then a deepening familiarity with life beyond limits will become clear to you, and you'll be at home and connected, whoever you are with and wherever you are.

CHAPTER 13

The Third CRAFT Skill: Attention

That Self is hidden in all beings and does not shine forth, but it is seen by subtle seers through their sharp and subtle intellect.

—Katha Upanishad 1.3.12

Our brain's capacity to direct, allocate, and prolong our attention is quite remarkable. Attention is important because it regulates and directs our mindfulness, which itself can move us to an expansive Awareness, and therefore to our fullness. Selective in nature, attention is constantly shifting; our curiosity and interest attract and reallocate it. Think of attention as a spotlight that illuminates specific aspects of what you perceive and causes everything else to diminish. It focuses on the object or task that is presently most significant and heightens your brain's engagement with it.

Although your mind most likely wanders and you might occasionally get bored, preoccupied, tired, or distracted, you

---

Go to http://www.newharbinger.com/40859 to listen to "Attention."

can probably get your focus back most of the time and intuitively alternate your attention accordingly. You may have had moments of complete absorption through intense concentration. Your mind was focused one-pointedly on an object, so much so that you became one with it. These are deeply meditative glimpses of clarity, harmony, and balance freeing our minds from the effects of desire and fear. In this state where the mind is no longer running the show but becomes a conduit for Awareness, there's the possibility of gaining ultimate insight into the deepest nature of both the mind and the object. This insight is of oneness and it's a gift of discerning focus—connecting with experience through being mindful and broadening our spiritual "vision."

Types of Attention

Paying attention draws on various levels of mental effort—we instinctively switch between these levels throughout the day. There are several different types of attention, all of which we use at any given time (Sohlberg and Mateer 2001). I hope that briefly exploring these experientially will show the dynamic capacity of your attention and expand your mindfulness beyond your sometimes relative, restricted perception.

Take a moment to direct your attention to a particular sound you can hear right now: perhaps the ticking of a clock, the sound of distant traffic, the chirping of birds outside, or another sound that makes itself known to you. This basic responding to stimuli is **focused attention**; it's your ability to attend momentarily by "tuning out" other stimuli. Now, move your attention to the felt sensation of the book as it rests in your hands and concentrate for a few minutes on this tactile sense perception. As this is **sustained attention** which requires a bit more effort, you may wish to close your eyes. When you open them, let your eyes rest on an object and fix your attention on it. This ability to filter out distractions and competing stimuli so as to select an object of focus is **selective attention**. Now, put the book down, stand up, and have a good stretch. Then, sit back down and get comfortable and continue to read. This ability to shift your attention back and forth between tasks is **alternating attention.** Finally, notice your ability to multi-task. Continue to read while inspecting the visual appearance of the letters and words your eyes are keeping pace with. Listen to the chorus of sounds around you, and check into the domain of taste and see if there's any residual flavor on your tongue from a recent drink or snack. This attending to multiple things in unison or rapid alternating attention is **divided attention.**

Attention can generally be divided into "volitional attention" and "non-volitional attention." Attention is *voluntary* when it's directed and fixed with our conscious effort. Usually, in this type of attention, we have an aim or desire in mind, and as a result, motivation plays a significant role. We, in our temporary guise as a finite, separate self, call upon and exercise our will. For example, sitting down to meditate and focusing our attention on our breath requires that we have a measure of discipline and concentration. Perhaps our goal is to de-stress after a busy day or to gain more happiness or well-being. With volitional attention, we try to control any distraction as best as we can, and our attention is directed to sitting, breathing, and observing.

Volitional attention is not spontaneous and not given so easily as *involuntary attention*. Involuntary attention comes without the play of will. When it's spontaneous, it's aroused through affection. We have no intention or desire to attend, but a bit like a reflex, we are at once compelled to move our attention to the object, idea, or person of our curiosity. There's no sense of individuality involved, no intellectualizing or conceptualizing (not in that first instant, anyway), only an effortless responding or "seeing." This sort of attention transcends itself and the seer in the process. I'm sure you can recall awe-filled moments when something unexpected caught your attention and took your breath away or melted your heart. In effect, spontaneously shifting your focus toward something striking, moving, tender, or remarkable can put your challenges in perspective and open you to your fullness. These moments are portals to Awareness (to Deep Knowing), where you recognize that all is One—the Aliveness seemingly outside of you is the same Aliveness within you. This is the unexpected end of duality.

Habitual attention is when our attention becomes molded by prior experience of something (Bruya 2010). Our response to that thing becomes habitual and we unconsciously move our attention toward it when it reoccurs. We cultivate this type of attention with the broadening and deepening of insight and, consequently, of what appeals to us. For example, a musician's attention might spontaneously be tuned to the background hum of music even while she is actively engaged in doing something. The same can be true for Aliveness; Aliveness resonates continually—can you hear it? Being nothing in particular, once you come to know Being, you'll discern it effortlessly, and you won't be fooled by the shallow play of duality. Such attention is Self-intimacy.

Attention Can Make Way for Awareness

Sensitively concentrating the mind so it's less judgmental and clingy is the essence of mindfulness. However, attention or concentration can only reveal so much to us because it has an onward focus and is limited; it's prone to getting divided and thwarted. Attention does, however, transmute into Awareness (Deep Knowing) when it meets and resonates with Aliveness in an object of meditation.

This deep absorption presents the realization of our complete connection and integration with and as oneness—the state known in Sanskrit as *Samadhi*, a state of one-pointedness naturally free of desire, fear, and imagination. In this stage of yoga, clear objectless universal Consciousness remains by itself as Awareness: Consciousness conscious only of its own internal nature, not of any external object. Thought has been

stilled and localized consciousness untangled from its embroilment with the mind. We recognize this clarity as our primordial existence, which is genuine love and joy. When we meet
one thing with Awareness, we meet all things. This is the
meaning of "*Namaste*."

CHAPTER 14

The Fourth CRAFT Skill: Fullness and Emptiness

"What is the origin of this world?" "Ether," he replied. For all these beings take their rise from the ether, and return into the ether. Ether is older than these, ether is their rest.

—*Chandogya Upanishad* 1.9.1

When we're asleep to the reality that separation is an illusion, our imagining, which is invariably colored by fear and desire, makes us think that never being enough or never having enough is the actual condition of life. This primary illusion not only shapes our experience, but it also becomes our experience, so we search for wholeness outside of ourselves within transitory people and objects. We become dissatisfied with our lot and feel lonely, deficient, and hopeless. Our glass is

Go to http://www.newharbinger.com/40859 to listen to "Fullness and Emptiness."

principally either half full or half empty of a bitter drink called "not-enoughness."

According to Buddhist teaching, the human mind in its default state, which I call restless inadvertence, produces *dukkha*—"unsatisfactoriness." The mind-made world never meets our expectations because it's a projection of our existential alienation and angst. Impermanence can't bring total or lasting satisfaction. This was a transformative revelation for the Buddha.

All Is You

We need to distinguish what is real from what is unreal, to debunk the illusory. When we earnestly question this way, we unveil an inner richness. We've touched on one approach— "mindful negation" or *neti-neti*, which loosens the hold of the mind by declaring "I am not the body, I am not the mind." Sri Adi Sankaracharya said that the Self is real and that the universe is unreal, but the universe is the Self. The universe is unreal because it's perceived and as such, imagined. If *neti-neti* is the negative method, seeing Self in everything is the positive. The universe is one creative manifestation of the Self, and the body-mind you call you and yours is another, so, as the Self, you're not limited to them and they don't ultimately define you. Each finite expression points to fullness yet each cannot contain fullness, just as a single snowflake cannot capture the vast snow of Antarctica. Existence originates from you (as Self, or Brahman), exists in you, and will return to you, declares the *Chandogya Upanishad* (a Sanskrit text which forms a portion of Vedanta philosophy). In other words, all is you.

Jean-Paul Sartre said that "existence precedes essence," which has become the generally accepted motto of the existentialist movement (Panza and Gale 2009). For Sartre, we have no predetermined blueprint; we simply exist, establish ourselves in the world, and only then do we define ourselves. Self-defining arises out of what we live, how we engage in the world. To exemplify this, the essence of a snowflake is water; a snowflake has an essence, but we don't. This is why essence-based metaphors aren't truly effective when attempting to explain our non-dual reality. Self isn't a material in the same way that water, gold, or wood are. Self can't be divided, because Self alone is.

There are no valid means for comparison or distinction; we can't compare two expressions of the same non-stuff. It just isn't possible.

Balancing Fullness and Emptiness

If our complete attention is on form, we end up identifying with it. Caught in the murkiness of dukkha, we feel stuck, fear death, and see ourselves as disconnected from our entirety. The flip side of the perceptual coin is this: intuiting nothingness might make us existentially anxious because we sense the absence of a solid center in ourselves. Angst is at the threshold of Being and Aliveness. To be aware of our existence involves facing the ambiguity of nothingness and freedom. Therefore, we might gain greater safety by becoming less mindful, but we'll also be less inclined to savor abundance.

Whereas *attention* is a function of the brain, *Awareness* is consonant with Self. Attention sees snapshots (usually selfies), and Awareness—Deep Knowing—sees the "bigger picture." Therefore, attention is essentially a means and not an end; it's a state of alertness which can let Awareness through. Awareness is the natural meditation of Being; since Being is the essence of all existence, it readily knows itself, and we can awaken to this. Awareness roots our minds and bodies to the ground of Aliveness, something no amount or quality of attention can achieve. Deep Knowing is that by which you intrinsically know Self. Prior even to Being, you are Self-aware.

We don't have to try to cultivate Awareness; we just need to inquire into how it gets obscured with restless inadvertence—with desire and fear-based patterns. We can boldly and mindfully open to the anxiety, fear, and desire we perceive, without trying to fight or escape. By being openly aware but not habitually defensive, we can see beyond the illusion of separateness and the suffering. By not being distracted by fantasies, we become present. This way, we are no longer limiting our experience with our agitated, muddled minds but resting in our natural state.

When we know ourselves as this pure Awareness, our mindfulness becomes more lucid and the details our senses meet become clearer and richer. With lucidity, we fathom the emptiness of the egoic dream for what it is—a play of our bountiful imagination enlivened by Awareness—Deep Knowing. The dream and the dreamer lose their sense of believability and significance because we see in perspective this moment's unfolding through the radiance of Awareness.

True emptiness is not a nihilistic nothingness that diminishes the dream and its forms, but a fruitful emptiness which makes the richness and fullness of life possible. Undoubtedly, form and emptiness are not independent; form can't be removed from emptiness, and emptiness cannot be removed from form (see the Heart Sutra, Sheng-Yen 2002). Ultimately, "emptiness" means being empty of an independent, short-lived separate self.

In open, wakeful Awareness, watch the rise and fall of thoughts. Observe how creation springs from emptiness. Thoughts appear from the unmanifested. They move through you seemingly at their own pace, and because they are as transparent as clouds, they recede into the nothingness from which they arose. Notice how silence is not at war with noise and noise doesn't actually reduce silence. The inflow of your breath which makes your lungs full of air doesn't compete with the emptying outflow. But there is one flow. Being changeless, undefined, timeless, and clear, you are the space of boundless potentiality. You are the unconditional love of what you manifest. Because of your emptiness, the world of fullness exists.

The river of life moves spontaneously, effortlessly, peacefully toward the unrestrained all-inclusive Source, and the mind is a conduit for its steady flow. The best use of the mind is when it gets out of the way and watches with interest. Then it will gradually be less likely to dictate or hamper the inevitable current. This is true mindfulness: the art of seeing beyond the *mind* (duality) to *fullness* (non-duality—which is so full, so all-inclusive it's also empty because it's All There Is). As we experientially assimilate the viewpoint of life seen from Deep Knowing and realize the essential perfection of every form and expression, we unite with and communicate that truth.

CHAPTER 15

The Fifth CRAFT Skill: Tranquility

Om. The heavens rest in peace,
   there is peace in the in-between.
   Brahman is peace, all is peace,
   peace alone is peace.

                    —The Texts of the White Yajurveda

I think of authentic contentment as imperturbability of our foundational sense of Aliveness. This has nothing to do with our usual entangled attempts at relative fulfillment or gratification. I resonate with the ancient Greek philosopher Epicurus's view that happiness is a question of tranquility or what he called *ataraxia*. To come to this conclusion, he wondered: If pleasure has to do with peak experiences, how should we differentiate the underlying foundation of subtle restfulness and well-being? This constant foundation, Epicurus

Go to http://www.newharbinger.com/40859 to listen to "Tranquility."

clarified, is the most profound pleasure of all, and we should try to stay aware of this ground of equanimity and be thankful for it (Christian 2001).

Tranquility is what's left when we stop being slaves to desire and fear; it's our natural state. We move our focus away from the things in which we invest too much energy that make us suffer, and dive back into the silent depths within ourselves. Because we're so familiar with and convinced by the almost tangible surface currents and have our sense of self invested in them, this might feel like a leap of faith into the unknown. We might at first experience this "diving" as existential loneliness, but as we surrender to it and trust Awareness to guide us, we encounter ourselves, transforming loneliness into radical aloneness. Here, we experience an extraordinary new confidence and calmness.

A Leap of Faith into the Heart of Aliveness

Shraddha is a Sanskrit term whose nearest English equivalent is "faith," although this isn't a brilliant translation (Easwaran 2007). "Conviction" is another loose translation. Shraddha literally means "that which is placed in the heart." When we take an honest look into our hearts, we find many unquestioned beliefs we've been holding onto for a long time. We can ask: "In what way do my fears and desires divert me from tranquility?" These structural beliefs form an unconscious map of reality which dictates our perception of ourselves and the world. As the Bhagavad Gita says, "A person is what his shraddha is" (17:3, Easwaran 2007, 63). Whatever we hold with affection and conviction becomes highly influential in our lives; it stimulates our action and shapes our behavior, leading us toward our idea of fulfillment.

We've crowded our hearts with limited beliefs that will never capture the wholeness of life, because inherent within every belief is desire and fear, but life is free of both. But through the radical discerning focus we've been exploring, our beliefs are held lightly or released completely and then our shraddha changes. Radiant peace dawns by first being mindful of the difference between the real and the unreal, followed by letting go of the unreal. Without this radical discernment and expansion of focus, the mind will continue to be seduced and hypnotized by what it imagines. But with discernment and focus, it surrenders naturally and becomes still as agitation and disturbance fade away. Not putting faith in the turbulent, aversive formulations our minds construct, we can be mindful of our immediate, direct Awareness of "what is" beyond belief. This is faith in its most authentic expression. It's a radical confidence in an existential holding that embraces and releases experience, making known a still space of undisturbed peace. Therefore, tranquility is what's left when the impermanent appearances of life inevitably fade.

Restless, inadvertent seeking is the antithesis of joy. Natural, clear seeing—or presence in Awareness—on the other hand, is the motionless way of contentment. Contentment is the continuous circular "road" of balance and stability on which the body-mind is held and travels. There is no destination except the journey itself, and realizing this brings great joy.

Integrating the Waves

This inner peace or deep tranquility is still but intensely alive. It's the silent depths of the ocean, and while the surface waves, always unpredictable, might continue to fluctuate, they leave the water below them unmoved. For this reason, I do not mean to imply that the anxious "waving" of daily life completely stops. I'm not describing never-ending happiness—there's no such thing. Happiness, like pleasure, is caused and has an opposite; it's conditional. I'm talking about the possibility of reconnecting or rediscovering, a depth of uncaused peace and joy below the craving mind. The main thing to see for yourself is that your Aliveness (the feeling "I am") is the same whether it's in an *apparently* restless form ("I am something/someone") or abiding in equanimity ("I").

In meditation, take a slow deep breath. Slowly scan your body and see if you can find at least one restful part and allow that restfulness to gradually permeate your entire being. Be aware of your whole body as best you can, gradually checking into each part and sensing how easeful or restful these parts are. You might feel Aliveness as energetic pressure, pulsing, heaviness, or lightness. Ask the restful parts: "What do you desire?" and "What do you fear?" Don't try to analyze, interpret, embellish, or reject any answers that come. Just let them be, holding them and releasing them as they dissolve. Sit with them for a while. Now scan your body again for any restless parts. Ask the restless parts: "What do you desire?" and "What do you fear?" Again, sit with any answers for a while. Is there any wisdom these areas hold for the restful areas? Finally, choose a restful area and invite it to spread its easefulness throughout your whole body. You might also ask a restful area to silently teach or offer the restless parts something for their greater good. Notice how alive, even neutral, both the restless and restful parts are, despite any stories attached to them.

Aliveness is your most loyal companion no matter what appearance it takes. You can reconnect with Aliveness by sensitively noticing your *Being*, both in rest and in action. Even your "waves" can serve as allies when given space to move and speak. When you rest in and witness Aliveness with tranquility, you'll encounter yourself as "something" beyond even Being or the witness (individual or universal). You're some nothing that cannot be verbalized or even experienced in the conventional sense. When you dive, you beckon an expanded Awareness which reveals truth: the wisdom and knowing prior to knowledge, "the peace of God, which passes all understanding." Yes, when truth dawns, you'll know yourself as not a mere body-mind, nor its animating Aliveness, but the Absolute itself. Having seen this clearly and directly, a calmness emerges, and infuses and saturates with love the "waves" of daily life. Because finally, it's obvious that there's no distinction between the waves and the entire ocean.

CHAPTER 16

The Sixth CRAFT Skill: Surrender

When all desires which once entered his heart are undone, then does the mortal become immortal, then he obtains Brahman.

—Brihadâranyaka Upanishad 4.4.7

According to the Bhagavad Gita, the most evolved and purest shraddha (meaning faith or conviction) is *sattvic*. When *sattva* (which literally means Beingness) is prevalent in us, the qualities of lucidity, tranquility, wisdom, harmony, discernment, detachment, joy, and peacefulness spring to life out of seeds of universal Consciousness. Transcendent of the ego's desire and self-interest, it's very different from faith that is blind or self-serving. Sattva is expressive and loving. It's a potent force which holds everything together by its energetic presence. Our Aliveness *is* sattva; in the heart of Aliveness, imagination is born which gives birth to self-expression and the adoration of truth. After all, Being loves to come out into the open and show itself. In doing so, the world of form is conceived, which as we know, gets mixed up with frantic wanting and rejecting as well as the many resulting identities. Our faith gets misplaced in false gods and idols. But the light of sattva continues to shine in the fog of obscurity.

Not-Knowing Is Clarity

Sri Nisargadatta Maharaj (1973) frequently enthused about the act of readjusting one's focus of attention to appreciate one's primary existence (which he often called I-Amness, Being, or Consciousness). By attentively inquiring into how the mind functions, its fear and desire-based motives, impulses, and associated identifications become evident. The false dissolves upon its discovery, Maharaj said. By surrendering what we are not, coupled with shifting to what lies beyond the mind, we come to an authentic *Awareness* of what we are. Of course, the mind cannot understand what is beyond itself, and this is why inquiry begins with not-knowing and concludes with not-knowing which is synonymous with Deep Knowing. It may sound ridiculous, but not-knowing is clarity.

Unlike the mind, Awareness is silent and non-dual. When the mind's analyzing and judging lose their prominence, it gives up its charge and recedes. The mind gives in and becomes supple, taking a break from unnecessarily consuming itself in defensiveness and seeking. With greater spaciousness and tranquility, the mind naturally meditates on truth, while its useful functioning continues to work in the background. This way, every moment of our daily lives can become a sadhana. As the mind becomes established in the Self, it frees itself from trying to grasp and escape from external things. Surrender, and indeed spirituality, is dying to all that we have inadvertently constructed for and through our limited sense of self.

Therefore, let's be willing to be completely honest with ourselves, to look at and release the precious concepts with which we've inadvertently built walls around ourselves. Let us push out past our acquired knowledge and be intensely interested in what is beyond the obvious.

We can do this by keeping the feeling "I am" in our minds and merging into it until our minds and feeling become one, as Maharaj advised. This "natural yoga" is the art of living in peace and harmony, with openness and love, an internal shift within our Aliveness which feels like existential surrender and sometimes existential angst. It's fulfillment by way of emptiness, a fulfillment that transcends all conventional fulfillments. It becomes apparent when we stop seeking to satisfy the inferred images of ourselves.

To be free of our false images, J. Krishnamurti said, we must be completely attentive to how they are built through our aversion and grasping. Total (that is to say, radically mindful) attention not only dissolves images into Awareness but actually prevents them, therefore allowing us to see without distortion (Krishnamurti 1973). Awareness, Krishnamurti said, is the total surrender to what is, without reason, without the duality of the observer and the observed.

Being Is Freeing

We're sattvic when our faith is in the formless God (universal Consciousness) of which seemingly localized consciousness is an expression. We see each expression of God as the force of oneness that connects the world of multiplicity to the universal God energy in all forms. Sattvic surrender is the end of egoistic authority: "my God," "your God," or even "me and God."

The blossoming of sattva takes continuous attention and cultivation, but in my experience it's more about clear focus than arduous labor. Because the quality of sattva is alive in us, we don't have to manufacture it, but attend to it. We can think of the body-mind as being like a garden, sattva as a bed of flowers, and restless inadvertence (desiring and fearing) as weeds and pests. Taking care of a garden takes constant devotion since like weeds and pests, our desire and fear are mental imprints or impressions which are rarely ever fully removed; they stay in a dormant state and therefore can become triggered at any time. But the more familiar sattva becomes to us, the easier it is to rest on it, to let go of trying to hold on and make peace with it—this is the path to real happiness. As we surrender and loosen our clinging to our beliefs and assumptions, the reality of our unadulterated Aliveness (which is inherently sattvic) is revealed. Rather than continuing to replenish our storehouse of karma (conditioned patterns of energy, thought, and behavior, along with associated unfulfilled desires and elusive fears) through restless inadvertence and indifference, we live meditatively and inquiringly with a heart of radical mindfulness. Gently investigating our storehouse, even if it feels painful or frightening, makes space for healing and righteousness. We find that our patterns don't define us, that our fear is due to estrangement from Self, and that our desire is actually a deep longing for Self. Only when this is seen does the karmic dream dissolve.

Don't struggle to relinquish anything; just discern emptiness and impermanence. Every form yields to the majesty of life. The individual can't let go; letting go is already happening. Surrendering is not a choice or practice; you *are* surrendered. Knowing this is true renunciation—it's the humble detachment from the results of fear-desire actions. To put it another way, surrendering is not an act of will. It isn't a passive submission but a wise and sane "handing over" to Self; it's a clear seeing of the actuality of the present moment.

Being at odds with reality, fear avoids surrender because it thinks that is a final death. Desire resists surrender because it sees it as ultimate dissatisfaction. We become afraid of disappearance, and we try to hold onto our imagined personality. This resistance to the normal ebb and flow of things is restless inadvertence. What fear and desire don't realize is that surrender is perfectly natural: evening surrenders to night, the caterpillar surrenders to the butterfly, breathing in surrenders to breathing out. Even the original embryo surrendered to become your body which will itself one day let go and transform. This deeper understanding of death is the start of true spirituality.

Spend some time contemplating other examples of natural surrender besides the ones I have provided above. You may wish to reflect on the material and intellectual possessions which you once held onto that have now become less significant.

PART 3

Alone with All: Natural Unity

CHAPTER 17

Seeing Clearly Now, Effortlessly

*Instead of trying to intentionally fix or improve "myself" or
"the world," I am more open to allowing everything to heal
itself in its own way, in its own time, as it does anyway. There
is a devotion to the immediacy of life exactly as it is right now,
without superimposing any kind of spin. This bare intimacy is
neither an effortful, goal-oriented, improvement-seeking
exertion, nor is it any kind of passive or fatalistic resignation.
It is an energetic aliveness, an openness that includes
everything and sticks to nothing. It is not something "you"
achieve or acquire, but simply the boundlessness, the bare
being that is always already fully present right here, right now.*

—Joan Tollifson, *Nothing to Grasp*

It's the habitual resistance to the normal fluctuation of life
that is restless inadvertence which obscures the simplicity
and lucidity of Being. It's the conditioned perception of unsatisfactoriness born from perceiving a dualistic world of deficiency which makes us feel fundamentally lonely, isolated,
incomplete, and insecure. Being the antithesis of joy and

empowerment, it's the concealment of the effortlessness and clarity of living.

Our inadvertent overlooking of Self and the suffering that ensues are an inside job. They obscure the mind and Being like a solar eclipse. An eclipse is a natural event, part and parcel of the arrangement and movement of the sun and moon; but what isn't natural is the belief that the sun doesn't exist when hidden from our sight. Similarly, our lack of discernment of and focus on our true Self and Source is a perverse (albeit unintentional) state. As a fleck of dust in our eye can cause irritation and haziness, so the erroneous belief "I am a separate, finite individual" demands our full attention with a single point of awareness, obscuring reality. We suffer from misapprehension, shortsightedness—that's all.

The antidote? To earnestly question if in truth we are confined to a dualistically isolated world of our own imagining, to take in the boundlessness of Knowing, and to uncover and inquire into the cause of our condition. Analyzing, numbing, or treating symptoms isn't enough.

From one perspective, desire and fear are foreign invaders that attack our hearts and serve only to cause psychic entropy and chaos. Seen with radical mindfulness, however, desire and fear are intended to achieve the thing we ultimately want: happiness—they just go about trying to achieve it in uninformed, "unenlightened" ways. They don't know that their very seeking causes the disturbance they try to evade or flee. When desire and fear take the steering wheel, they pursue happiness through chasing or avoiding and take us down the road to unhappiness. This hapless driving sways us from one direction to the other. When desire and fear (or the separate individual) are no longer the drivers, we find that life moves itself perfectly. Life becomes an enchanting journey into a familiar mystery.

What is needed is discerning focus, the opposite of restless inadvertence—the blend of skills and qualities of Self-inquiry and meditation organized in the mnemonic acronym SEER CRAFTS. Inadvertence clouds; discernment makes clear. Glimpsing the mechanism of our bondage—self-identification with the impermanent—calms the relentless surge of desire and fear. And so, liberation is nothing other than having clarity about this. There's no other way to effectively relinquish desire and fear unless we expose their roots to the loving light of Awareness, our foundational Deep Knowing. All else is crisis management. Expanded Awareness and receptive discernment rectify our "vision"; they calm and purify our minds, revealing to us what we are.

It's sometimes difficult to fathom, but the mind is like a clean and steady lake which reflects absolutely anything on its surface without distortion. Reflections can appear, but the water is untouched. This clarity is the natural condition of the mind, the perfect state to effortlessly meditate on the Self no matter what the body is doing. The mind that has assumed a discerning focus is a discriminating one—not discriminating in the relative sense of judgment about things in the world; absolutely not. It is discriminating in the sense that we unmistakably identify Aliveness (through negation, for example) in everything and that no thing can divide or limit Aliveness. A gift of this focus is that we stop identifying with the imaginary and step out of its fear-desire cycle.

From Emotional Reactivity to Clear Responsivity

What I'm attempting to describe is not the opposite of loneliness (or any other mood, experience, or emotion); radical mindfulness *includes*—or compassionately embraces—loneliness and all other suffering without getting enthralled to them. In other words, we know loneliness (and its isolated victim) as just one dualistic focal point of attention in the boundlessness of Awareness that we are.

In being out of sync with ourselves, however, we're shut off from what's truly happening, and our ego stories ("I'm not enough," "I'm inferior," "I'm superior," etc.) are compelling and all-consuming. Our chattering minds influence much of our day—our actions, reactions, and emotions. We're often hypersensitive to the drama around us in an alien world, and our eyes are closed to any common ground. The world rarely conforms to our hopes because it's a projection of incongruence, a projection which takes lots of energy and effort to maintain but no energy whatsoever to transcend.

To be free of this projection's unnecessary limitations, look with clarity at the separate self. Try to observe its comings and goings, the way it arises and dissolves, and the desires and fears it consists of, until your seeing is purer and your discernment greater. Be mindful of ego-based thinking, reacting, interacting, and acting. Of course, there's nothing wrong with emotions—all are valid—but isn't it beneficial to everyone to be mindful of impulsive, emotional outbursts that erupt from a place of fear? Without eruption, or indeed suppression, we can tenderly hold emotions in mindfulness, intending not to harm. What we accommodate in our Beingness and give space to gets transformed, thus freeing our energy and calling forth tranquility. And so with a tranquil, earnest mind, free from emotional reactivity, our spiritual "eyes" are purified; we meet life as it is, with clarity and compassion.

Inattention obscures; attention clarifies. Clarity of mind and heart enables us to meet the challenge of impulsive reactions that we regret later—we can avoid acting from a basis of insensitivity and disregard. Our greatest challenge, at least on the experiential human level, is to live, behave, think, feel, and act in harmony with reality instead of ego. Ultimately, no effort is required; it's just a subtle shift in focus from inadvertence to discernment. It's discerning that each relative happening is the direct result and the flawless expression of the Absolute. Each relative happening is in fundamental synchronization with the Absolute. Our suffering is the outcome of living in experiential discord, of living on the surface of lives led by desire and fear. But we can perceive reality from the vantage point of this absolute perfection, this greater order. Even though we're often in the habit of complicating it, reality—truth—is evident, all-inclusive, and accessible to everyone.

Our humanness is a perfect expression of reality. Just as it takes a bird no effort to be a bird, it takes no effort to be human; our humanness does its own thing while the body-mind functions according to its particular quirks and inclinations, however we may feel about them. Because their idiosyncrasies are involuntary, even the most "awakened" people may catch themselves in unenlightened emotional and mental habits from time to time, but when caught they're quickly released. Even the most intense anger, for example, subsides into stillness as Being is brought to the forefront, that is to say, as the mind becomes calm. Being is always aware of Self and offers a reliable tether to a relaxed mind. Difficult emotions dissolve only on reconnecting with something as peaceful and eternal as Self. In doing so, we learn to stop being ruled by our internal state when an external event triggers us. We understand that life flows freely; it's only our short-lived self-concepts—ego identities—that create the experience of bondage, and even these identities have a "flow" about them when seen.

This doesn't mean we don't cry or laugh, but in staying connected, we have a capacity for detachment and are grounded in clarity and calmness. Detachment, in this sense, doesn't mean apathy or disengagement; it means we can step back and appreciate the spontaneity of our reactions. We consequently foster a friendliness with the entirety of experience—internal and external. So, ironically, detachment creates harmony between both domains. Yes, if we want a more peaceful and unified world, our bodies and minds must mirror these qualities.

In being watchful and not getting tangled up in reactivity, we don't give the flames of emotion any extra fuel. Stepping back is a key part of mindfulness and a giant leap toward freedom. For example, we're less likely to seek out or relate to others out of an inferred place of neediness or deficiency, or indeed superiority or control. We get to meet the neutrality of the world and our body-minds when we're not in the grips of clouding mental states that would otherwise manifest in harmful actions. What we hold in mindfulness cannot hold us.

We can step back from the things that make us agitated, to put aside the stuff that perturbs our underlying tranquility. In doing so, we tap into our inherent wisdom and live in alignment with it. This is the way to honesty, integrity, and wholeness—all of which ingredients are essential for happiness.

The Source Flows Through All Without Effort

As we release our stories of aversion and attraction, we meet the present moment with a lucid and gentle responsiveness. If we dare to look and surrender, or rather realize that we are *already* surrendered, we rise above the fictions we have created for ourselves. Then, we start to effortlessly love what is without expectation and encounter our infinite potential. This radical mindfulness is the moment-by-moment clarification and focusing of the mind; it's a way of relating with the full scope of our experience through being mindful and broadening our spiritual "vision." Being aware this way, we realize that whatever is present has a rightful place for no other reason than because it already is here, whether the mind likes it or not!

Our potential, as the Source, is always flowing through everything with no effort because it isn't trying to become or reach a point; it just *is*. Think about the last time you were effortlessly involved in an activity—when you were "in the flow." You could enthusiastically attend to whatever you were doing, even the mundane tasks. Maybe you even experienced a heightened sense of things, and perhaps lost all sense of time, too. To the degree that you're aware of your natural ease, the seemingly insignificant things are seen to be unthinkably extraordinary. Likewise, even the things that we once labeled "undesirable" or "fearful" take on a fresh relevance.

When our seeing is unconditional and receptive, we're easily able to stay with whatever arises, even if there's a passing superficial wish for things to be different. Without being dominant or distracting, that desire and any connected thoughts and feelings are purely part of what the greater order permits. Because we're friendly with and interested in our experience, our Beingness accommodates the seeing.

You can be aware of your effortlessness now by giving attention to your breathing. Notice how the body knows exactly how to move and regulate the in and outflow of air. Neither strain nor effort is involved. Observe it, and you'll get a sense that breathing happens by itself without "your" involvement. When thoughts arise, don't follow them or identify with them, just let them go; the mind is following its own pattern, doing its own thing, and you can witness it and return your attention to your breath. You're seeing without special effort; it just happens; you're not even *being* the seer. This seeing and attending can apply to any happening—inside and outside the body-mind. Observe the spontaneity of your words, thoughts, and actions. Even control and will are spontaneous happenings. Whatever you can experience (internally or externally) you're not limited to or restricted by. This includes your small sense of self along with its various components, habits, and qualities, and any other experience.

As you get familiar with and grounded in the essence of all experience—your essential Beingness—dispassion toward these expressions occurs spontaneously. This is an unforced letting go, not an intentional one. And as your preoccupation with the body-mind softens, you are united with your natural Self. This release of identification—which is completely normal, spontaneous, and actually inevitable—is true freedom. Just be, living life as it unfolds with radical mindfulness.

Idiocentric moods and patterns may continue to come and go, but we can allow ourselves to feel into them with detachment without telling stories about what they mean. This seeing invites spontaneous, intelligent, kindhearted action. Fortunately, once even a moment of clarity is allowed to shine, the eye of Awareness never fully closes. This shift in focus makes the mind clear; nothing has to change except our focus and attitude.

There is a life that lies beyond the laws of conditionality and linearity, beyond time and space, beyond the dualistic stories we tell ourselves. Woefully, we hide this life from view by guarding against the extinguishing of our individuality. We are that very life. You need only realize that none of the masks are your actual face to distinguish between the real (the unlimited) and the unreal (the limited). Facades aren't needed. Thus, in nakedness, be radically mindful of your Self and you'll rediscover your exquisite, original face, and renew your natural state of connectedness. This is the objective of mindfulness: to liberate us *now*, in our present-moment experience, from the illusion of separation, to reveal our true value and immensity, to, as the Buddha said, overcome our sorrow and lamentation.

CHAPTER 18

Marrying Life

In this purity, without qualifications or form, even the concepts of the witness and the witnessed, of the mirror and its content, must dissolve.
We may call it bliss, as nothing can disturb it.
We may call it total acceptance, as nothing is rejected by it.
We may call it unconditional love, as everything is embraced by it.
This magnificent simplicity, this open secret, this intimate clarity is all there is. It is yourself welcoming you home. You are this.

—Leo Hartong, *Awakening to the Dream: The Gift of Lucid Living*

Welcome to your wedding day, your exquisite unity with life. Are you surprised by the unexpected commencement of this special ceremony? Perhaps you're suddenly feeling unprepared, restless, uneasy, nauseated, overwhelmed, half-hearted, pressured, or out of sync. Believe it or not, you were always engaged to, in, and with life. Everything up to now has led to this moment of marriage, of joining and integration with your countless expressions as the One Life. This book has hopefully served as a wake-up call. Can you hear the wedding bells?

Anxiety is normal; it's okay to have cold feet, but know you need not feel bewildered, forlorn, or afraid. Fear is a result of believing life to be unfamiliar and divided, remember. All you need to do is show up, be present, and have trust. These are your only vows. Will you be with your own Self, listen to it, obey it, cherish it, and keep it in mind always? You intuitively know how to respond; just stay attentive and interested, and let Self-love dawn. This sacred occasion will happen (or rather, is going on right now) quite effortlessly and spontaneously—it helps to notice this. It's a ceremony of harmony, peace, friendliness, and love, divinely consummated by an intimate yoking with the dynamic stillness within that is your Self, climaxing in a merging with the Beloved.

This marrying of life is a natural yoga. The word "yoga" comes from the Sanskrit verb "to yoke"—in the sense of a device joining one thing to another. In yoga what is yoked is our attention, which left unchecked, typically flits from one thing to another. The age-old purpose of yoga was to unite the individual self with the ultimate Source: Brahman (Hamilton 2001). Because the multifaceted world, populated by diverse beings and phenomena, is an expression of the Absolute, yoga was presented as a route back to the Absolute, the One Self. Accordingly, what's essential is to discriminate between that which is eternal and that which is non-eternal and to dwell on, or meditate on, our sense of Beingness as a portal back to the primordial heartbeat of life.

At the core of yoga is the extraordinary insight into an ordinary reality that transcends limitation and suffering. As we've been finding out, our restless inadvertence distorts and diverts us from a clear seeing of reality. Yoga is a practice by which localized consciousness gets untangled from the mind and the imagined world, resulting in greater harmony and wisdom. Ultimately, all yogas conclude in the marriage of localized consciousness to life.

In his book *I Am That*, Sri Nisargadatta Maharaj describes Nisarga Yoga as living life with "harmlessness," "friendliness," and "interest," abiding in "spontaneous awareness" while being "conscious of effortless living." "Nisarga" means natural, innate, inborn, and spontaneous. The vital apparatus for this simple yet powerful "art of living" is to delve into the knowledge of "I" to reach its Source (Nisargadatta 1973, 173).

A natural yoga implies that we are already connected with our Self because it is the Source, and that clarity, reality, and freedom are at hand. To put it into action, we try to see clearly, from wholeness, and seek to relate with authenticity and harmlessness. Nisarga Yoga, which we could call "natural unity," is about being awake to the effortlessness of Aliveness, living in spontaneous Awareness (or Deep Knowing), discerning with focus—being radically mindful of what is so. Because we inherently *are*, our Beingness is our freely given unity with life. The only practice is to Be and to affectionately bring Awareness to that Aliveness to let it reveal its truthful Source.

The dream was that you were astray from the universe; the reality is that you *are* the universe and there is nowhere that your Aliveness isn't. All is you; therefore all is well.

Making Peace with What Is

Life often seems random and chaotic, and sometimes misaligned with our desires or needs. The ego thinks it is supreme and that everything should comply with its viewpoint and purpose; it can never be peaceful and harmonious because it's the opposite of peace and harmony. Part of its nature is an unwillingness to be one with life and a refusal to live in alignment with the inevitable. If it saw that it was one with life, it would instantly perish because its pseudo-existence is based on separateness and it likes it that way. Thankfully, the ego isn't a permanent entity and its insubstantial nature offers openings to a greater order.

When I say "greater order," I'm not describing a higher purpose removed from the human paradigm; I'm pointing to life's unavoidable "isness" or intimate actuality. Events are inevitable, though they're not preordained by an egocentric, aloof God. This greater order is not something mysterious or nebulous; it's this *here, right now*—this flawlessly emerging moment we're married to. With a radical quieting and focusing of mind, we can feel it, see it, smell it, taste it, and hear it in everything, wherever we are. We can realize that we are always in alignment with it because we *are* it. Such a realization transforms our expectations to work with reality, and teaches us that although events may not unfold as we expect, there's a certain equanimity in honoring the inevitable. When we allow this insight in a natural and unforced way, a profound peacefulness amid the imagined duality communicates itself to us as our unshakable Aliveness. A changeless tranquility, an unqualified gladness become evident amid the mind's habitual judging. It's all-pervading perfection that dawns when life is seen through the lens of Being instead of through the intellect. This insight, this clear seeing is the only real way to make peace and uncover genuine connection with the One Life.

"Non-duality" doesn't mean "against duality"; it's not meant to imply that duality is bad. "Anti-duality" denotes a dualistic state of mind from whence springs the fraught pursuit of certain expressions of life and the turning away from others. In other words, non-duality is both the Deep Knowing of inseparability and an entire embrace of passing paradox. It's the supreme balancing of the contraries. It's authentic connection. It's Self-realization. It's unconditional love.

There's a profound open secret to real, lasting peace: to want only what we presently possess and to not be concerned about what we are yet to possess. Because you are all that is, essentially, you want everything that happens within the illimitable space that you are. There are no outside authorities or villains to blame or punish for doing things to you against your will; it's all done by you to you. For this reason, the sooner you admit your authorship, that on some level you desire and create your every experience, the sooner you won't feel so lost, isolated, and afraid. Being honest with yourself will help you align with what's true. You are one with life, nothing is apart from you, and knowing this is sanity. Even when you don't know it, you are living and therefore loving yourself in your countless manifestations. So, accept your marriage vows and take responsibility for them, warts and all.

Pure love, the unmanifested Source, willed you into Being and your Being gives life to every yin-yang life expression. The same will created desire and fear, and you led yourself to think that you want particular expressions (people, objects, self-concepts, experiences) over others. Your isolation and loneliness were always rooted in seeing yourself—that is, life—through the distorting filters of desire and fear. Self-alienation may have led you to avoid interpersonal separation and to attempt to fill the perceived gaps in your life with possessions and busyness. Again, I say "Self-alienation" because estrangement is an inside job; there's no external force doing this. I tenderly encourage you to forgive yourself.

Make peace with what's present; it's easier than you might think. But here's the caveat: peace is the end of the separate self. Why? Because the individual operates in a discordant, resentful state of imagined fragmentation. The individual doesn't have the capacity to contain the wholeness of existence—even though it tries its hardest to by embracing acquisition and aversion. This "push-pull" game obscures tranquility, and fulfillment seems to exist elsewhere—in the past or future, anywhere but here. But *what is* is already in harmony with life. Contentment is the imperturbability of our essential Aliveness which is currently flowing with the "isness" of this moment. Each manifestation of life is compatible with every other manifestation. Your existence, your wholeness holds everything with more than enough capacity and compassion. Appearance is acceptance, remember. There's no point in resisting what is deeply accepted. In being rooted in wholeness, authenticity and peace are possible. Even your desire for things to be different can be met with clarity and compassion. By meeting the present moment with radical mindfulness, you'll become more and more able to align your responses with the love and peace inherent within your fullest Self.

If this is all difficult to swallow, firstly know that you need not take my word for it, and secondly, check it out in your direct investigation. This means being sincerely curious about the implications of what I'm saying and courageously letting go of old beliefs and assumptions. Curiosity together with courage is a powerful response; it means being wholeheartedly receptive to truth without distorting it. Most importantly, it means spending some quality time with what is, and even more so, delving into your sense of Being and trusting it.

Put down this book, get quiet and focused, and do it now. With openness and looseness, witness your mind's innocent disposition to jump to conclusions and its desire to seek answers. Shine awareness on how these mechanisms create conflict and agitation. See how the pursuit of peace causes unease. Observe how the mind gets stuck in the compulsion of judging, avoiding, and

grasping, and how it tries to assert control. Notice how it creates
suffering by turning ignorantly against its Source.

The very watching of the mind slows it down. When it's
still, it naturally meditates on Being. Be mindful of the difference between the real and the unreal, and the indescribable
truth that you are will remain. In doing so, an intimate familiarity with yourself beyond imagined limits will become
obvious, and you'll feel peacefully at home in a natural,
unforced way. Along with this is a built-in compassion—a
capacity to relate affectionately and sensitively to what you
observe.

Outward events—relationships, work, leisure—go on, but
inwardly we quietly witness. The more deeply aware we are,
the richer our joy. An inner attitude of nonresistance and
tranquility, together with courage and patience, reveals the
perennial Source of true happiness. While the body-mind has
its characteristic desires and fears, Deep Knowing—
Awareness—is uninhibited and unshakable. It's always lucid,
serene, and bright.

Without needless resistance, we naturally live life with
ease, lightness, and spontaneity. We don't feel we should be
elsewhere, doing something different, or try to be someone
we're not. Obviously, we can easily imagine better conditions,
fantasies about how things "should" be ideally, or how others
"ought to" meet our expectations. However, our work is not to
construct utopia, but to be kindhearted and lucid with life's
"isness." As Ajahn Sumedho said, "For the awakening of the

heart, conditions are always good enough" (Kornfield 2008, 369). Everything we need—acceptance, courage, patience, understanding, compassion, mindfulness—is inherent within this moment. We have all the ingredients necessary to discover freedom and love exactly where we are.

We're no longer dependent on attaining more or fighting what is because we know life will happen as it will regardless of our dependency, desire, or fear. There's an equanimity and a Self-love in remembering this truth. Because we discover that genuine happiness is spontaneous and effortless, the objects, people, and conditions we once depended on are now lovingly released. We allow ourselves to love and to be loved.

Through recurrent moments of Self-intimacy, we can awaken to our inherent worth beyond the limits of the body and its personality. We can trust our worth and express it through the daily sacrifice of desire and fear. We can remember that we are independent of desire and fear and even existential angst. They arise in us; we do not arise in them. When we are radically mindful, we can discern and focus on lucidity and love.

Our minds flourish in clarity and ease when we take time to abide in the notion that we are not limited to or defined by the body-mind—we are free. This freedom means that we are not defined by its personality or its needs or even by the observer of these. Experientially (as opposed to absolutely, since there's nothing for Self to do), clarity cleanses our desires and makes our actions charitable. This inner refinement reveals an unimaginable depth of truth and love not divorced from the "isness" of life.

The clear seeing of our dilemma—that of restless inadvertence—is both surrender and liberation. Let us take the courageous, motionless journey to the space of pure Awareness, where Aliveness remains in wholeness prior to it becoming tainted as something in particular. Once we dip our toes in our Source, we easily and continually discover it wherever we are.

CHAPTER 19

Radically Alone

In taking ourselves to be a separate entity we have come adrift from our homeground, and inevitably fear and desire arise. In compensation we pursue happiness and security and try to escape pain and sorrow.

It is only when we understand the illusionary nature of this projection that we become open to our real nature, that which is beyond the mind. The Self is not something new to be attained, for it ever is; it has only to be recognized.

—Billy Doyle, *The Mirage of Separation*

We yearn to stop our loneliness and our overwhelming sense of incompleteness. We organize our lives around back-to-back blocks of interaction, stimulation, and distraction. We'll even tolerate acquaintances we don't particularly like, feeling that it's better to be distracted in company than to face the abyss. Living our life in this way is often chronic and debilitating; it suppresses the blossoming of Self-realization and our strength and abilities because we have an outward-looking, lack-driven focus. Self-alienation and estrangement lead us to fear being alone and unconnected and make us overdependent on others. And the desire to put an end to incompleteness typically ends up intensifying our isolation.

Sui, a university lecturer, describes much of her twenties as a period of darkness, plagued by a pervasive sense of insignificance. Feeling like a boat drifting aimlessly in a dark ocean without an anchor, she was painfully lonely. Utterly disconnected, not only from the people around her but from life itself, it was as though the universe or perhaps God had abandoned her. "The life I once knew before this period seemed like a dream, a mirage on a distant shore—one that I desperately clung to but could no longer fully grasp," she reflected with me. "I was floundering but no one noticed. All I had was my deafening, blinding, all-encompassing existence. The world went on, indifferent to my desperate struggle and quiet disillusionment. I felt like a fugitive, dislodged from time and space, directionless, meaningless, and absolutely forsaken." Sui was lonely even amid company and despite having achieved a successful, fulfilling career. Loneliness was a fundamental basis of her life—and of all human life, she realized.

We are compelled so forcefully to subscribe and conform to the inherited world of meanings, to conventions and to norms, to ascribing meanings and attachments to life, that our sense of Beingness is rendered inauthentic and becomes concealed. Even as we hunger for oneness, paradoxically, we war against it by acquiring and achieving, and this causes us a great deal of suffering. It's a contradictory game of wanting not to want. Seeking to seek no longer. Desiring to be desireless. Avoiding and removing the things that don't match what we seek. In such a predicament, we can't help but feel existentially lonely, anxious, and incomplete.

For Sui, it was this insight and acceptance of the fundamentality of loneliness that became a turning point. The darkness she had become so uneasily accustomed to gradually became revelatory and purifying. Instead of seeing her existence as a flaw, she found acceptance. She started to embrace her sense of abandonment and release her need for a cast-iron anchor. With detachment and curiosity, she found the capacity to hold her emotional patterns without trying to analyze or fix them. The detachment described here is not about escapism, avoidance, or rejection; it's our compassionate capacity which holds dualistic phenomena rather than being held by them.

Sui had assumed her unease was rooted in her lonely childhood, being raised as an only child by her grandmother who reluctantly assumed the caretaker role when her parents were both too busy trying to make ends meet. While not ignoring the reality of her past, she asked the questions "Who am I beyond my identities?" and "Who is it that knows these painful memories?" Not getting a definite answer, she rested for some time in the darkness of her existence—her sense of Being—and stayed as receptive as she could. To her surprise, through being attentive, Sui uncovered a source of tranquility. It was a tranquility so potent she could feel it in her body— like in her solar plexus, which had been eclipsed by years of tightness and contraction—as well as know it in her being. "By deeply surrendering to my separateness and investigating it as best I could, an inauthentic way of living became unmasked, blowing asunder my mistaken, limiting attachments to the world and to my self-concept as a lonely person."

We're coaxed into a false consciousness that is meant to give us a sense of ontological security. Alienated, we are strangers in our own lives, strangers in a world of otherness, uncertainty, and death, and no one can help us figure out our strange, forlorn existence. Can there be a lonelier predicament? Our willingness to be with our angst may just uncover a lightness of Being. Beneath our self-made dualistic existence lurks an existential anxiety, the abyss of nothingness that threatens to annul our attachment to all that we strive for. But this nothingness is not a threat. It's the threshold of a truer state of Beingness—Aliveness.

Far from being comfortable, anxiety, as I've described above, has the power to liberate us, unearth awe-inspiring insights, and dissolve our perfect fantasies. This means anxiety and loneliness leave us "unclothed" and defenseless, but this is a bountiful state for valuable discovery. That is to say, living from an ongoing stance of fresh and dynamic inquiry and meditation means looking at life and ourselves, beyond surface appearances.

Our tranquil foundation has always been present; the vast sky has always been there. You've been overlooking the setting because you were fascinated with the buildings or the stars— the "structures" of your inner and outer environment which comprise characteristics, concepts, qualities, values, beliefs, activities, habits, and mental imprints or impressions. Structures crumble. Stars eventually die. You're the primordial foundation, not the ideas you have about yourself; they too will fade.

Aloneness Is Oneness

As we've discovered, the impetus of the universe is desire: the desire to be and for experiential Self-intimacy. Before being sensed locally by the body-mind, Aliveness is universal; it is All There Is. As such, Aliveness could also be called oneness. This all-inclusive wholeness has neither individuality nor a distinct body or mind; it's all bodies and minds. Out of oneness comes a unique body-mind and consequently comes the play of individuality, but the body-mind and its localized Aliveness is never cut off or alienated from the whole of life. Because your oneness is All There Is, you are always alone—radically alone—but not necessarily always lonely.

This universal Aliveness spontaneously arises in a body-mind, among other forms, and starts expressing itself. The ego (a bundle of desire and fear) gradually claims that Beingness like a parasite, and starts to infer in duality a separate self with a personal existence which needs reinforcing and defending. The individual becomes seemingly divided in duality—*in-divi-dual*—thereby disguising oneness as the egoic mind. One manifestation of this is the assertion "I am someone/something in particular." Notice how the ego bypasses the "I am" part of this Self-knowledge. The "I am" is so close, but being constantly preoccupied with desire and fear, the ego can't handle this Aliveness. "I" perceive myself to be dualistically isolated, deficient, and sometimes existentially lonely. Therefore, we must inquire into the nature of this "I"—to liberate it from its false imprisonment. This process is what spiritual inquiry and meditation boil down to.

When what is boundless becomes apparently restricted to a distinct form, the suffering—fearing and desiring or aversion and attraction—begins. Ego projects a broken world of otherness, aversion, and lack. The pure I-Amness shared by all gets veiled and we inadvertently seek a way back to wholeness. We are the whole universe but we think there's something else outside us. Between us and our true home, time and space are imagined, confusingly creating a multitude of routes, maps, and guides.

When we know that we exist not merely as a human being but as oneness, there's a possibility of discovering our radical aloneness—our seamless unity with life. In wholeness we lack nothing. Existence, being One, is you and yours; there is no one and nothing else. You're radically alone and your aloneness is simultaneously empty and full—in the fullness of company or the emptiness of solitude.

The Personal Is Impersonal

We identify ourselves by saying "I" or "me," unconsciously representing an assumed personal existence, but when we realize that we're not limited like this, we recognize ourselves as the One Life. Your body is a marvellous biological expression which wouldn't appear without life energizing its perpetual formation and endurance though the spark of imagination. It's not that we own and eventually lose a share of Being—Being is all-inclusive, as all-inclusive as water, light, and the sky. Personal expressions arise and dissolve, but oneness is constant. Beingness is what we are; not personal Beingness, but impersonal Beingness which is oneness. In reality, every person's sense of Being is compatible with every other sense of Being because Being is One. The entirety of all perceivers is the oneness of Aliveness. Aloneness is oneness—the all, alone. There is nothing individualistic about Aliveness; it has a "nature" of sorts, but not a personality. Every mode of life, from individuality, localized Beingness, to oneness and the Absolute, is one expression.

Waking Up to What Is

Without inquiry, the fictitious continuity, permanence, and solid self-concept that are the projections of your imagination will continue to be compelling, given meaning by the filters of desire and fear. All these compelling stories depend on drama infused with moments of equilibrium and disequilibrium, yin and yang. You're so used to existing in this conceptual prison that you've blindly assumed it has to be this way, but I'm here to tell you it doesn't. Discriminating between the real (the unlimited) and the unreal (the limited) will reveal to you that you're already inseparably connected to the One Life. This is liberation from dualistic imagination, as the great spiritual teachers have told us for centuries.

To realize "our" oneness, we need to earnestly question the duality we take for granted and be receptive to the word-less truth that remains. When we've had enough of our suffer-ing to have realized the usual fixes don't work and become sincerely curious about other possibilities, we can't help but open our eyes to wholeness. When we find the courage to be the *letting go* and live in harmony with what is, in oneness with life, we go beyond the need for routes, maps, and guides and realize that we've been searching for home *within* home. We wake up to the reality that duality is in imagination only and wholeness is actual. We can use the skill of attention to tune into Aliveness habitually; when we do, our self-Consciousness becomes universal Consciousness (oneness), shifting us from existential loneliness to radical aloneness. Not only can we observe Aliveness in formal meditation; we can find ourselves held securely and compassionately within it in everyday life.

All we're ever searching for is Self-intimacy. We want to encounter ourselves wholeheartedly and relax deeply into our Being. Once we know that we are the world and that the world springs from our consciousness, we are simultaneously liberated from desire and fear and become entirely responsible for every manifestation and event. Desire and fear may visit, but we disidentify with them as soon as we witness them, making true forgiveness and love possible. Our witnessing or seeing takes place from the unrestricted unfolding of oneness whose vision comes from the Self. This radical mindfulness is Self-intimacy.

"I'm always at the precipice of nothingness, of emptiness, and that's okay," reflects Sui. "I can live with that now because there's also the flip side which gives balance and form to the void. I wanted the light to break through the clouds of darkness. Deep down I always knew the sun was there. But in allowing and questioning my shadowy isolation, I could prepare the foundation for something amazingly expansive and illuminating. Yet this was not a one-off process. Rather, it's a perpetual and at times frustrating renewal of courage. It calls forth my fortitude to constantly let go of my fake guises, and passionately embrace life in all its absurdity." Sui's outlook was transformed when she had the bravery to contain opposites—to be everything and nothing. To give our unconditional presence to the paradox of all modes of life is to hold the key to true connection. We must remain undefended to touch the unknown, to open to wonder, and abide our suffering and angst—to expand our existential vision and permit our extensiveness. This is the art of living the life that we are. When, like Sui, we have the courage to be unified with the "isness" of this moment, to be with whatever comes, we might discern that life—our radical aloneness—however different it is from our beliefs and expectations.

CHAPTER 20

Mountains and Valleys

Mountains and valleys are one flowing event that cannot be pulled apart. Sages have called this the One Self or the One Mind. This all-inclusive and undivided unicity is all there is, and all there is, is this. Seeing through the illusion of separation is an essential realization on the pathless path of liberation. At the same time, it is obvious to anyone that apples are not oranges and that mountains are not valleys. Thus, the truth is said to be not one, not two.

—Joan Tollifson, *Nothing to Grasp*

As our mindfulness blossoms and we expand our focus, our identification with a finite body-mind loosens, and our feeling of immediate Beingness transmutes into oneness. Then aloneness isn't an experience of lack or deficiency; it's a direct meeting of what we are. This is the way to healing, to Awareness, to unity. There is a fine line between Aliveness and aloneness.

Explore your sense of Aliveness with mindfulness and you'll sooner or later notice that your observing core is much vaster than you assumed; it's as encompassing as the space within and around everything. When you think you've found the origin of your observing, you can dispassionately step back once again and investigate the preceding layer of observation. When we see without approval and disapproval, the Beingness of all things becomes the Awareness (Deep Knowing) within and beyond all things. Keep inquiring like this until there isn't a fixed position—until your "eyes" are not only wide open but All There Is, until Deep Knowing is All There Is. This will help you awaken to your full Being as the single seer. First, become good friends with your vital Aliveness. Get to know it and it will tenderly lead you to your Source by freeing you from your provisional identity as Aliveness or oneness. If you're earnest, you'll realize that you are oneness, and you can't suffer—only the phantom ego-self suffers—for there is nothing outside you to inflict pain. Not because of the mind's analysis or its conclusions, but by responding to life meditatively and inquiringly will you awaken to this. Aliveness itself will take such a stance and Deep Knowing—Self-awareness—will dawn.

With this Awareness, this Deep Knowing, you might say in utter surprise: "Everything is myself!" or "Nothing is myself!" because the images that once depicted a separate "thing" no longer define you, or set you apart from anything else that is "not you." But even within this Deep Knowing, there seems to be the recurring appearance of an individual grounding sense of "me" which makes it possible to continue to function in the world.

In the body-mind, Self is echoed as Knowing and felt as Aliveness. Aliveness can recognize itself and discern its wholeness; Deep Knowing cannot look at itself because it isn't dualistic—its vision transcends the seen and the seer. The aloneness of oneness, albeit radical, suggests an opposing state of connection or relationship, both of which infer a connection between two or more entities. "Advaita," a more accurate term to describe the non-duality of Deep Knowing, means "not two." It's for this reason that the word "oneness" (and all words) can only take us so far in this exploration of life. No expression of life is final.

Mountains Are Valleys, Valleys Are Mountains

Both individual Aliveness and the universal Aliveness are but two expressions of the indefinable Source; even the phrase "non-duality" can't do it much justice. The dualistic universe doesn't bind your unlimited Self, and so it transcends relative concepts such as exclusivity and inclusivity. It dissolves every container; it passes through every barrier. It's not even "loving" in the way we think about love; there's no possibility of intimacy because the lover and the loved are not two. Oh, the irony of *radical* intimacy!

My favorite Zen saying attributed to Ch'uan Teng Lu depicts this beautifully: "Before I had studied Zen for thirty years, I saw mountains as mountains, and waters as waters.

When I arrived at a more now intimate knowledge, I came to the point where I saw that mountains are not mountains, and waters are not waters. But now that I have got its very substance I am at rest. For it's just that I see mountains once again as mountains, and waters once again as waters" (Watts 1957, 126). At the end of our investigation, there's an *appearance* of a "me" along with a world of diversity.

When we remember that we are the Source of the world, we're aware that we are the unconditional love of its conditional appearance; that Self-remembrance is to love and to love is to remember. The fearlessness to be radically alone is our ability to be authentic, to be what we are in our entirety. Focus on your original Self, offer faith, and it will emerge. Tethered to your Self (not your self-descriptions), you'll no longer see yourself as desolate or small. As you turn within like this, you'll notice that only the body-mind is limited and only its imagining finite, while the unbounded life that you are is you and yours.

We cannot become what we are. But we can recognize it. It's just a matter of focus, clarity, and discernment. In recognizing duality, Self alone remains. Know yourself as that, and be that. Even just a glimpse of oneness will prime you to return home to Self. This isn't a journey but a moment-by-moment seeing that takes place at home. Likewise, I'm not pointing to a special state of consciousness; it's big-Self-realization which is ordinary and ultimately inevitable because there is and never was an individual! This clear seeing is sort of a "non-event" because the eternal Source never truthfully was in bondage to its fleeting manifestations. Similarly, one doesn't get married merely to experience one's wedding day or honeymoon; they're just short-lived events that signify something even more special. What most matters is the everyday integrated, loving life that transpires after the ceremony and celebration. We don't try to bypass the anxiety of Being, nor do we lose ourselves in desire and fear. While desire and fear obscure it, anxiety, if allowed, uncovers the truth of what we are, by revealing our Aliveness to us as a trustworthy guide.

We know that anxiety is a common response to liberty, and an unavoidable insight into not-knowing. The angst of living compels us to inquire, creating shifts of awareness which unveil the freedom to be exactly as we are. No longer avoidant or passive, we're sane and lucid and recognize that everything takes its natural course. There's no need to reject our humanness, nor to go on believing that we are limited to our human expression. We don't mistake our impermanent expressions for our permanent Source. Embracing and living the life that we are, we're awake to our infiniteness while deeply in love with our relative manifestations.

When desire and fear don't ruffle our mind, we briefly find our identity as the pure witness—the seer. We can then step back from both the seen and the seer. Witnessing is a link between the diversity of Aliveness and Deep Knowing of the Absolute. In spaciousness, we rest into Deep Knowing. Then, there's only dimensionless seeing, or unconditioned Awareness in which reality is recognized. We are the Absolute—we can't avoid living it—but we also permit ourselves to view ourselves through every mode of life. No matter the mode and its limitations, there is only one eye. Self needs no seer, no understanding, no assurance. It *is*.

All That Remains Is Deep Knowing

From the start of our journey together, you've been actively questioning the beliefs and ideas you've previously taken for granted. You've been surrendering what you are not, and shifting to the truth that lies beyond your mind. You have an authentic Awareness of what we are. I know this because you've never been able to avoid truth completely, because it's All There Is! Your mind can't comprehend it and that's fine. Remember, inquiry starts with not-knowing and ends with not-knowing, which is synonymous with *Deep* Knowing.

Courageously shifting our focus of consciousness from knowledge to the state of not-knowing unfolds a space for fresh insight to present itself. Hence, the end of dualistic isolation requires us to get through the barriers that anxiety represents, to say yes and recognize our expansiveness. From here, the future is a presently appearing story unfolding in the space of now. Grounded in the immediacy of our Being, natural intimacy with life can awaken.

Not-knowing is the foundation on which the conceptual arises and falls. Continue to question everything to see through your mind-made assumptions. Shifting your focus from concepts to not-knowing clears a space for wisdom. This isn't resignation or passivity; it's a Self-remembering which lightens the mind's analyzing and judging—a wakeful resting into truth. Nor is it a quick fix; it's an uncensored, courageous embrace of what is. It's about naturally allowing the appearances of life, while not getting trapped in or identifying with those appearances. To hold and release what appears, to make peace with this moment's unfolding, is the path to happiness and fearlessness.

In Deep Knowing there is complete unity with the present moment, absolute accord with life as it unfolds. There are true abundance and security at the heart of life; a calm, clear, compassionate space that sees through but that isn't dismissive of difference and conflict. The door is always wide open to every hungry and scared soul; each can find nourishment and comfort, as there's always ample room and affection. Life asks nothing of us but to open our eyes and hearts to its gentle invocation, to mindfully seek within ourselves and to remember our sacred birthright. This rediscovery opens a "new" world of endless possibilities and subtleties never before imaginable. To repeat: you are no-thing, no particular concept, no fixed idea the mind can conjure, and this is wonderful news. Knowing this truth is wisdom. You are pure potentiality; you have the capacity and freedom to be anything and everything. But never forget: no expression can capture your fullness.

Please don't take my word for it; I'm no more special than you. Inquire for yourself, as yourself. Encounter yourself. Be present with yourself, your most intimate Aliveness: look at it, listen to it, embrace it, surrender to it, return to it continually. This is an effortless letting go rather than a desperate attaining. It's experiential, not intellectual. An openness rather than a narrowness. A Self-remembering as opposed to self-improving. It's truly *Being*, not a passive sleepiness but a wakeful and kindhearted relaxation into uncensored and alive truth.

What's particularly helpful in living the life that we are is a gentle yet engaged presence in all circumstances. We rest as surrender, no longer attempting to swim against the flow, and the waterway leads us home. Yes, it's possible to let the water of life stream through us with loving attentiveness and spacious observation while being fully human—in times of both beauty and terror, as life unfolds. This presence is Aliveness. It arises when we transcend our ideas about how life "should be." Our goal, our home, is no longer a distant state, but a radical way of seeing.

Discover, be curious about and watchful of the river of Aliveness and let it guide you to your supreme Source. It's through becoming mindful of the full significance of Aliveness, and going to its birthplace prior to Aliveness, that we can realize our true authenticity, which transcends time and space, subject and object, birth and death. Your focus and clarity of attention are all that need to change. The qualities and skills for your new discerning focus are in your hands. May you find the courage to become more profoundly attentive, to expand your vision to new levels of Aliveness, and to actively engage in the wondrous, ineffable life we share.

The SEER CRAFTS skills can guide you to your own Beingness. And your own Beingness is your most trusted teacher and friend; it will never leave you. Life is the greatest guru, the finest teacher and teaching, and you are living it perfectly just the way you are showing up right now. Everyday life will continue, but you're in touch with your most loyal companion, connecting you to your original home. So you don't feel isolated and alienated from life, from yourself, locate and keep coming back to your Aliveness. You can't go wrong. Just don't be distracted by your desires and fears; merely see them as passing scenery. Despite appearances, you're always on the right track, exactly where you're meant to be. You can't *not* live the life that you are.

Our time together doesn't have to end here. Do keep listening to the special radically mindful "soundtrack" I've composed while you continue to investigate, reflect on, and assimilate what we've been sharing. Go to http://www.newhar binger.com/40859 to access these tracks. Also, please visit the website for this book where you can read my SEER CRAFT blog and learn about the facilitated inquiry sessions I offer: http://www.thelifethatyouare.com.

References

Annamalai Swami and D. Godman (ed.). 2000. *Annamalai Swami Final Talks*. Tiruvannamalai: Annamalai Swami Ashram Trust.

Balsekar, S. 1982. *Pointers From Nisargadatta Maharaj*. Durham, NC: The Acorn Press.

Blomfield, V. 2012. *Gautama Buddha: The Life and Teachings of the Awakened One*. London: Quercus.

Brach, T. 2013. *True Refuge: Finding Peace and Freedom in Your Own Awakened Heart*. London: Hay House UK Ltd.

Brown, B. 2010. *The Gifts of Imperfection: Let Go of Who You Think You're Supposed to Be and Embrace Who You Are*. Center City, MN: Hazelden.

Bruya, B. 2010. *Effortless Attention: A New Perspective in the Cognitive Science of Attention and Action*. Cambridge: The MIT Press.

Cacioppo, J., and W. Patrick. 2009. *Loneliness: Human Nature and the Need for Social Connection*. New York: W. W. Norton & Company.

The Campaign to End Loneliness. 2014. *Alone in the Crowd: Loneliness and Diversity*. The Calouste Gulbenkian Foundation. https://gulbenkian.pt/uk-branch/publication/alone-in-the-crowd-loneliness-and-diversity/.

Christian, J. 2001. *Wisdom Seekers: Great Philosophers of the Western World*, vol. 1. Belmont, California: Wadsworth Publishing.

Denton, J. M. 2015. "The Texts of the White Yajurveda." In *Gems of Advaita: A Sanskrit Reader with Selected Significant Philosophical Excerpts from the Upanishads, Bhagavad Gita, Vivekacudamani and Others. Word by Word Transliteration and Translation*. CreateSpace.

Doyle, B. 2008. *The Mirage of Separation*. Salisbury: Non-Duality Press.

Easwaran, E. 2007. *The Bhagavad Gita (Easwaran's Classics of Indian Spirituality)*. Tomales, California: The Blue Mountain Center of Meditation.

Foundation for Inner Peace, and H. Schucman. 2007. *A Course in Miracles*. New York: Penguin Books.

Gaitonde, M. 2017. *Self-Love, The Original Dream: Shri Nisargadatta Maharaj's Direct Pointers To Reality*. Mumbai: Zen Publications.

Gangaji. 2013. *Hidden Treasure: Uncovering the Truth in Your Life Story*. London: Penguin.

Greven, J. 2016. *Oneness: The Destination You Never Left*. Salisbury, UK: Non-Duality Press.

Hagen, S. 2012. *Buddhism Is Not What You Think: Finding Freedom Beyond Beliefs*. New York: HarperCollins.

Halifax, J. 2007. *The Fruitful Darkness: A Journey Through Buddhist Practice and Tribal Wisdom*. New York: Grove Press.

Hamilton, S. 2001. *Indian Philosophy: A Very Short Introduction (Very Short Introductions)*. Oxford: Oxford University Press.

Hartong, L. 2016. *Awakening to the Dream: The Gift of Lucid Living.* Salisbury, UK: Non-Duality Press.

Kierkegaard, S., and A. Hannay (tr.). 2015. *The Concept of Anxiety: A Simple Psychologically Oriented Deliberation in View of the Dogmatic Problem of Hereditary Sin.* New York: Liveright.

Kornfield. 2008. *The Wise Heart: Buddhist Psychology for the West.* London: Ebury Publishing.

Krishnamurti, J. 1973. *The Awakening of Intelligence.* London: Krishnamurti Foundation Trust Ltd.

Lumen Learning. 2016. "Plant Responses to Light." Boundless Biology. https://courses.lumenlearning.com/boundless-biology/chapter/plant-sensory-systems-and-responses/.

Madhavananda, Swami. 1921. *Vivekachudamani of Sri Sankaracharya.* Dt. Almora: The Advaita Ashram, Mayavati.

Maharaj, Sri Nisargadatta. 1973. *I Am That: Talks with Sri Nisargadatta Maharaj.* Durham, NC: The Acorn Press.

Maharshi, R., and D. Godman (ed.). 1991. *Be As You Are: The Teachings of Sri Ramana Maharshi.* London: Penguin.

Maitri, Sandra. 2001. *The Spiritual Dimension of the Enneagram: Nine Faces of the Soul.* New York: Penguin Putnam Inc.

Merton, T. 2005. *Contemplative Prayer.* London: Darton, Longman & Todd.

Moustakas, C. 1961. *Loneliness.* Upper Saddle River, NJ: Prentice Hall.

Müller, M., trans. 1879. *The Upanishads, Part 1 (SBE01).* http://www.sacred-texts.com/hin/sbe01/index.htm.

Müller, M., trans. 1879. *The Upanishads, Part 2 (SBE15)*. http://www.sacred-texts.com/hin/sbe15/index.htm.

Lawrence, D. H., 1930. *A Propos of "Lady Chatterley's Lover."* London: Mandrake Press.

O'Donohoe, B. 2005. *Sartre's Theatre: Acts for Life*. Pieterlen: Peter Lang Publishing.

Osho. 1988. *The Book of Women: Celebrating the Female Spirit*. New York: St Martin's Press.

Panza, C., and G. Gale. 2009. *Existentialism for Dummies*. Hoboken, NJ: Wiley Publishing.

Park, J. 2015. *What Is Spirituality?* James Leonard Park—Free Library. https://s3.amazonaws.com/aws-website-jamesleonardpark—-freelibrary-3puxk/CY-JOY.html.

Red Pine. 2008. *The Platform Sutra: The Zen Teaching of Hui-neng*. Berkeley, CA: Counterpoint Press.

Robertson, F. 2017. *The Art of Finding Yourself: Live Bravely and Awaken to Your True Nature*. Oakland, California: Non-Duality Press.

Sankarâchârya. 2012. *The Crest-Jewel of Wisdom and Other writings of Sankarâchârya* The Freedom Religion Press.

Sartre, J. 2004. *The Transcendence of the Ego: An Existentialist Theory of Consciousness*. Oxfordshire, UK: Routledge.

Sekida, K. 2005. *Two Zen Classics: The Gateless Gate and The Blue Cliff Records*. Boston: Shambhala Publications.

Sheng-Yen. 2002. *There is No Suffering: A Commentary on the Heart Sutra*. Berkeley, CA: North Atlantic Books.

Sohlberg, M., and C. Mateer. 2001. *Cognitive Rehabilitation: An Integrative Neuropsychological Approach.* New York: The Guilford Press.

Thompson, M., and N. Rodgers. 2015. *Understand Existentialism: Teach Yourself.* Blacklick, OH: McGraw-Hill.

Thorne, D. 2005. *Sphurana: The Yoga Practice of Atma Vichara, Its Context and Method.* Bath, UK: Yogaliving Ltd.

Tillich, P. 2014. *The Courage to Be.* 3rd ed. New Haven, CT: Yale University Press.

Tollifson, J. 2012. *Nothing to Grasp.* Salisbury, UK: Non-Duality Press.

Victor, C., S. Scambler, J. Bond, and A. Bowling. 2000. "Being Alone in Later Life: Loneliness, Social Isolation and Living Alone." *Reviews in Clinical Gerontology* 10: 407–417.

Watts, A. 1957. *The Way of Zen.* New York: Pantheon Books.

Yalom, I. 2008. *Staring at the Sun: Being at Peace with Your Own Mortality.* London: Hachette Digital.

Yao, X. 2010. *Chinese Religion: A Contextual Approach.* London: Continuum International Publishing Group.

Nic Higham is a certified counselor, life coach, and a practitioner of neurolinguistic programming and Ericksonian hypnosis. He has over ten years of experience working for the National Health Service (NHS) in mental health inpatient care and a therapeutic community. Higham leads a number of mental health service improvement schemes, run by a UK-based charity whose work aims to enhance the lives and autonomy of marginalized social groups. For a number of years, he has been actively involved in communicating the message of non-duality through organizing seminars, producing popular podcasts, blogging, and managing social networking platforms. Higham is a mindfulness tutor at a recovery college, where he teaches people with emotional and mental problems, as well as health care professionals. He lives in Leicestershire, UK.

Foreword writer **Scott Kiloby** is an author, a licensed Indiana attorney, and a California Certified Addiction Treatment Counselor. Cofounder of The Kiloby Center for Recovery in Rancho Mirage, CA—the first US addiction treatment center to focus primarily on mindfulness—Kiloby is also co-owner of the Natural Rest House, a detox and residential center in La Quinta, CA. He is COO of MyLife Recovery Centers, a nationwide treatment program providing the naltrexone implant. In addition, Kiloby is founder of the Living Inquiries Community, a mindfulness facilitator training program with approximately one hundred certified facilitators who work in over twelve different countries. He regularly speaks at conferences, seminars, and workshops on mindfulness, spiritual awakening, and legal and ethical compliance in addiction treatment.

MORE BOOKS for the SPIRITUAL SEEKER

ISBN: 978-1626258716 | US $16.95

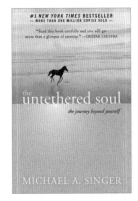

ISBN: 978-1572245372 | US $16.95

ISBN: 978-1684030156 | US $16.95

ISBN: 978-1684031344 | US $16.95

Register your **new harbinger** titles for additional benefits!

When you register your **new harbinger** title—purchased in any format, from any source—you get access to benefits like the following:

- Downloadable accessories like printable worksheets and extra content

- Instructional videos and audio files

- Information about updates, corrections, and new editions

Not every title has accessories, but we're adding new material all the time.

Access free accessories in 3 easy steps:

1. Sign in at NewHarbinger.com (or **register** to create an account).

2. Click on **register a book**. Search for your title and click the **register** button when it appears.

3. Click on the **book cover or title** to go to its details page. Click on **accessories** to view and access files.

That's all there is to it!

If you need help, visit:

NewHarbinger.com/accessories

new harbinger
CELEBRATING
40 YEARS